BREAKING
FREE

FROM THE SHAME OF

Addiction

BREAKING *FREE*

FROM THE SHAME OF

Addiction

AMANDA HARMS, M.A.

CFI
An imprint of Cedar Fort, Inc.
Springville, Utah

ISBN: 978-1-4621-4509-6

Published by CFI, an imprint of Cedar Fort, Inc.
2373 W. 700 S., Suite 100 Springville, UT 84663
Distributed by Cedar Fort, Inc., www.cedarfort.com

Library of Congress Control Number: 2023934965

This is not an official publication of The Church of Jesus Christ of Latter-day Saints. The opinions and views expressed herein belong solely to the author and do not necessarily represent the opinions or views of Cedar Fort, Inc. Permission for the use of sources, graphics, and photos is also solely the responsibility of the author.

Cover design by Courtney Proby
Cover design © 2022 Cedar Fort, Inc.

Printed in the United States of America

10 9 8 7 6 5 4 3 2 1

Printed on acid-free paper

To Timothy Harms for providing
much knowledge and wisdom,
The Recovery Village at Palmer Lake for helping
me grow in my knowledge of addiction,
Ginger McGovern for the idea of a workbook,
and especially my husband Matthew
for his patience and love.

Contents

Introduction

As a member of The Church of Jesus Christ of Latter-Day Saints, I was raised with the gospel standards and morals that God has set forth from the beginning of time and into the last days. The adversary is working extra hard and with serious overtime in these last days to veer us away from living these Gospel standards. As a society, we are dealing with a pandemic of mental illness and addiction. We learn that addiction is "bad" for us, yet, more and more people continue to become addicted to various substances. Think about it, as a society, we are more addicted than ever.

The problem is that as members of the Church, the Lord encourages us to keep the commandments, including refraining from some of the most addictive substances such as alcohol, drugs, pornography, and gambling. However, sometimes the pain of being human and the rush of getting a fix to numb the pain becomes so strong that we don't just want the fix, but we *need* it. After we get the fix, the wash of shame comes over us with an *"I'm not worthy"* attitude. This feeling of unworthiness leads us to believe the thought, *I am not worthy*. As we agree with this idea, we allow it to reinforce a belief of unworthiness, thus dragging us down further into our shame. It becomes a cycle of using substances, feeling shame, and then using substances again because of the shame. It doesn't seem to end.

As a counselor who works with people who have addictions, I wanted to write this book to help those who are members of the Church to break free from their shame and hopefully help end their addiction. It is my hope for you to better understand how one can break free from the binding grip of shame. I not only want you to understand, but to know how to put into

1

practice the skills and tools I have found to be helpful with my clients. I also want you to be able to better understand and put into practice the enabling power of Jesus Christ. I am hoping you will be able to feel His great power in your life and the love He has for you personally.

Thank you for taking the time to read this book. By following and practicing its principles, you will be on the right track to break free from your shame of addiction. Many blessings to you and to your new journey of change.

Chapter 1

Introduction to Shame and Addiction

The shame of addiction, especially as a member of the church can be debilitating. You desperately want to be the best person you can be, but shame is pulling you in the opposite direction. It hurts so much that there are times you feel you don't deserve to go on. Addiction can be a terrible partner in life, and the shame you feel because of it tells you you're not worth it. I know a little bit of how you feel as I have worked with many clients who feel the shame of addiction. The good news is that there is hope of breaking free from shame and becoming the person you are meant to become.

As a counselor, I worked at a substance abuse treatment facility where I would facilitate a group on shame and vulnerability. I used material from Dr. Brene Brown, a psychologist who studies shame and vulnerability. I have my clients write down what makes them feel shameful surrounding their addiction. We discuss their shame in a group setting, but later I would read everything they wrote. I have been brought to tears a few times as what they write is gut wrenching. I had one client explain his experience with alcohol. He drinks to forget and numb the pain from war. He wrote of a young man who was scared to fight, and my client made him get out and fight. The young man was killed soon after. The shame my client feels is too much to bear at times, so drinking helps him numb the pain.

Before I truly begin this chapter, I want to mention that whenever I write *use* or *drug use,* I'm referring to all illegal drugs, addictive prescription drugs, alcohol, pornography, gambling, shopping, gaming, food, etc.

Actually, anything can be an addiction if it's causing relationship problems, financial problems, health problems, and/or spiritual problems.

There are many reasons why we become addicted and stay addicted, but for most of us humans, it comes down to if we feel we are worthy of love and belonging. Everyone wants to feel loved. Everyone wants to feel like they belong. Dr. Brown has researched this topic for many years. In her book *Gifts of Imperfections,* Dr. Brown wrote, "Shame is the intensely painful feeling or experience of believing that we are flawed and therefore are unworthy of love and belonging" (2010, p.39 as cited in Brown, 2007). Basically, shame says, *I'm not worthy of connection or love and therefore I need to crawl into my little hole and numb the feelings.* We use because we want to numb ourselves. We don't have to feel, because feeling shame, embarrassment, sadness, or any type of pain, just plain sucks. The problem though with numbing the pain, is that you numb all the good emotions too. "We cannot selectively numb emotions. When we numb the painful emotions, we also numb the positive emotions" (Brown, 2010, p.70). You would be surprised at how many of my clients have epiphanies when they learn they numb all their emotions when they use. It makes sense, right?

When we talk about shame and the feeling of *not being enough,* we are talking about connection with our family and friends. "Connection is why we're here. We are hardwired to connect with others, it's what gives purpose and meaning to our lives, and without it there is suffering" (Brown, 2012, p.8). The shame that comes from addiction and feeling as if you are not enough can be so binding that it becomes a cycle. You feel shame about yourself, (perhaps you're not perfect enough or smart enough or talented enough) and then you use drugs in order to numb the feelings that come from shame. Dr. Brown describes shame as a warm wash that comes over a person. It can take form in all sorts of negative feelings such as anger, embarrassment, disrespect, hurt, sadness, despair, etc. After numbing for a while, you begin to want connection—because you're human—and so you begin to reach out, but wait, you start to feel vulnerable and realize, *I'm not worthy of love and connection because I'm not perfect enough or smart enough. I'm going to numb myself.* It becomes a cycle that drags you deeper and deeper into your addiction. If you've ever watched the TED Talk, *Everything You Know about Addiction is Wrong,* by Johann Hari, you would know that he says, "The opposite of addiction is not sobriety, the opposite of addiction is connection" (TED, 2015). Connection is why we are here.

True connection involves healthy relationships that are built upon trust, assertive communication, commitment, and, most importantly, unconditional love. In addition, true connection constitutes responsibilities that require time, attention, and the feeling of being wanted and needed. These positive connections enable a person to feel loved and important. Conversely, it might be you are trying to connect with your addiction because you do not feel worthy of true connection. Obviously, this is a false sense of connection, which leads to feelings of unworthiness and shame. We may ask ourselves, *Then why am I connecting with my drug of choice?* Because connecting with your drug is so much easier than connecting with a person. Your drug of choice doesn't judge you in any way. It accepts you for who you are and says to you that you are worthy to be its best friend no matter what. It gives you an out from all your cares, worries, and problems. It says, *I am here to keep you safe from all the negative feelings you are experiencing. I will be your friend and never forsake you.* As a human being, you need connection. If you feel you aren't worthy to connect/bond with another human being, then you will bond with something, even if it's detrimental to your life. It is how our brains work.

Now that I have explained a little about the cycle of shame and addiction, I want to touch on the subject of feeling shame as a member of the Church. Shame in the culture of religion and spirituality has played a huge factor in how we have treated our fellow man. If you look to the past, you can see how shame has been used as a social control mechanism. It is a way to make people conform to the culture that has developed. Think of the book *The Scarlet Letter* by Nathaniel Hawthorne (1850). Here is a story of a woman, Hester, who was forced to wear a scarlet-colored letter, an "A," on the front of her dress. The "A" represented adulteress. Hester was forced to stand on a scaffold for three hours so that the townspeople could shame her. Hester ended up wearing the scarlet letter for the rest of her life. This is what we call social control; a way to make people conform to their cultural norms. Although this story is fictional, it is based off true accounts of people being shamed in that culture. Shame is intended to "make" people conform to the said cultural standards. The only problem is that it does not work. People who are shamed will either conform out of fear rather than respect, or they will rebel, become apathetic, or sink into despair. They generally will not say, *Oh yes, you're right. I'm sorry I did that,* and then fix the problem. Drawing upon your own recollections of mistakes you have made, have you felt shamed by others? Have you complied with others' standards when you were shamed? If you did, did you feel good about it afterwards? I would say, "No, you did feel good." You probably felt resentment toward that person, or perhaps you were afraid of them.

The social control of shame happened to me recently. Due to circumstances at work, we were asked to sign a document that stated rules/guidelines that I was incapable of following. I chose not to sign the document because I didn't want to compromise my integrity. I spoke with Human Resources and after trying their best to get me to sign, the department representative resorted to shame. I was told it was my obligation to abide by these guidelines if I was working in healthcare. Other shaming comments were also made. At first, I felt bad but then realized I was being shamed because I would not conform! I decided I was not going to allow those words to poison me. Sure, I felt bad about the situation, but I didn't feel bad for maintaining my integrity. There is a difference between shame and guilt; they are not the same thing. Guilt is "I'm sorry I messed up." Shame is "I'm sorry *I am* a mess up." I will explain more about this in a later chapter.

Shame has been used for centuries and has been passed down from generation to generation. Shame is no stranger to the LDS culture. Our ancestors who first joined the church were probably Protestants, Methodists, or Baptists. Many of these religions stem from the Puritan churches that used shame as a way to get people on the "right track." These religions shaped our ancestor's way of communicating—a maladaptive way of communicating, nonetheless. Our great-grandparents and grandparents and parents were all raised with shaming techniques that were intended to help them conform to the cultural norm. Have they passed these on to you? I hope you are beginning to see how you may have been shamed in your own family. I'll admit it. I have shamed my husband and my children. I am trying hard to change my own ways and not shame anyone. Learning about shame helps us to recognize when we are shaming and when we are being shamed. This can start the process of breaking free from our own shame by building healthier connections with others.

I am going to tell you flat out–shame is from the devil! The adversary wants us to feel shame. Why? Because shame breeds disconnection. The adversary wants you to disconnect with others and reinforce the belief, *I am not worthy of love and belonging.* He wants you to isolate yourself so he can bring you down to his level. On the other hand, God does not want you to isolate, but rather connect with Him. God does not want to shame you, but rather pull you out of shame and love you into wanting to make changes in your life. God is your Father in Heaven. He is the perfect Father who loves you more than you know. Sometimes we don't feel or believe we are worthy of His love, and yet, He loves us anyway. Satan wants to make us feel shame and God wants us to feel Godly sorrow so that we will repent and turn to Him. I don't know about you, but I prefer the latter.

Let us bring this topic back to the Church and how we as Church members handle the shame that comes from others, especially from members of the Church. Let's face it, we've all experienced shame. Dr. Brown writes in her book, *Daring Greatly*, that if you don't feel shame, then you are probably a sociopath. If you are reading this book, you probably are not a sociopath, which is a good thing. If you're wondering what a sociopath is, think of a narcissistic person who has no empathy. However, I digress. I think you'd agree that the LDS culture is different from mainstream Christian sects. Many Christians do not believe in the Godhead the same way we do. This is important to understand because it depicts the nature of God and who He truly is as a Heavenly Father. He is our Heavenly Father, Jesus Christ is our perfect brother and Savior, and the Holy Spirit is the Spirit of God that testifies to our spirits that Jesus is the Christ. They are three distinct individuals yet unified as one in purpose. This is essential to recovery, by understanding that the only way to have communion with God the Father is through His son Jesus Christ, His Atonement and His Great Love. I will speak more about this later. The point I'm trying to make is "we know that it is by grace that we are saved, after all we can do" (2 Nephi 25:23). We do the best we can in this life, but ultimately, it's the love of our Savior and His grace that allows us to live with Him. As members of the Church, sometimes we feel that we have to be good, and if we aren't, we deserve to be shamed and feel unworthy of love and belonging. This is a false concept because God knew we would make mistakes, and Jesus suffered and died for us so that if we repent, we don't have to feel shame for what we have done. If you feel like you are not worthy of love and belonging in the church or maybe even within your family because you can't follow the "rules," try to understand what Brad Wilcox wrote in The Continuous Conversion, "We are not earning a treasure in heaven, but learning to treasure heavenly things" (2013, p.23). I like to look at it as us "learning" our way to heaven. This life is about progression and working on learning how to be like Christ. When we allow Satan to spread the warm wash of shame over us, we begin to digress, and hence create a bigger chasm between us and Jesus. Again, shame breeds disconnection.

Moreover, people with an addiction need to understand how to break free from shame, or as Dr. Brown calls it, *Building Shame Resilience.* I want you to know that even though you have an addiction, there is no shame in it. Yes, addiction draws us away from our Savior, and we need to work towards drawing closer to our Savior. This means your addiction must go in order for you to continue learning your way to Heaven. *But I've already tried, so many times,* you say. I get that, believe me I do. Removing your addiction is not easy, it is a process, and if we can remove the shame behind your addiction, then you are one step closer to breaking free! I am going to help you in this process of breaking free from your shame or as Dr. Brown calls it, building shame resilience. Please know that it will take a lot of self-reflection and work, but I know you can do it!

Chapter 2

The Neuroscience of Addiction

Before we truly get into shame and how to break free from the shame of addiction, you need to understand how and why you are addicted. If you already know how the brain interacts with addiction, you may feel the need to skip this chapter but please don't. All of us need to be reminded of things we have learned to help ingrain them into our brains. Also, if you don't understand how addiction affects the brain, then please pay extra attention to this chapter. I feel this chapter helps set the foundation for our understanding of addiction and how to break free from shame.

First, I just want to say that addiction is partly genetic. In fact, according to Dr. Melemis, "Addiction is due 50 percent to genetic predisposition and 50 percent to poor coping skills" (Melemis, 2020). My Grandpa is from Austria and, as you may know, beer is a huge part of the culture. Grandpa loved his beer, but he gave it up when he decided to fully engage in the gospel. However, Grandpa did not give up his sweets, and later became a diabetic. I remember my mom telling me once (before she knew about genetics being a part of addiction) that if she drank alcohol she would be an alcoholic, so she was glad she didn't drink. Still, mom was a "sugaraholic" like her father and ended up having diabetes which is a predisposed genetic disease. With that said, it is important to think about your ancestry and how that plays a role in your addiction.

There is an age-old question that people have been asking for decades about addiction. *Is addiction a choice, or a disease?* You may have your own opinion, but having been in this field for a while, I am a firm believer that addiction is at first a choice and then it becomes a disease. So, yeah, it's both.

If you have an addiction, you may feel sometimes that your addiction is controlling you rather than you controlling your addiction. Your cravings and urges to use can become so intense and strong that they turn into an actual *need* to use substances rather than a want. Basically, you feel *compelled* to use. With this compulsion, making a choice not to use brings up more anxiety within yourself, insomuch that you need to use just so you can release the urge or anxious feeling. Your mind says, "No!" But your brain says, "Oh Yes!" It becomes a conflict within yourself, and a lot of times your brain wins the battle. Why doesn't your brain listen to what your mind is trying to tell you?

I am going to get a bit technical here, but I feel it's really important to understand the science behind how addiction affects the brain. Please, bear with me. The brain is made up of billions of cells called neurons. Each neuron controls the pathway of information from one neuron to another via neurotransmitters. Each neuron contains a receptor that accepts the neurotransmitters from the other neuron. The neurotransmitter attaches to the receptors, sending a message from one neuron to the other, which then will send a message to another neuron and so on, until the message is sent to where it needs to go. Think of a track and field relay race, passing the baton from one runner to the next. The race goes like this: The team is made up of four runners (or 400 billion neurons). The first runner has a baton in their hand. The starter pistol fires (stimuli to the brain), and the runner dashes off as fast as he or she can sprint. They catch up to the next person, who is running at this point, and pass off the baton to that person. The first runner is the neuron, the baton is the neurotransmitter, and the next runner is the receptor who then becomes a neuron. It's good to note that the neurotransmitters are eventually pulled from the receptor back into their own neuron by transporters. This cuts off the signal from the neuron.

When dealing with substance use, substances interfere with the process described above. Certain drugs can make the neuron release more neurotransmitters than usual or interfere with the transporters. Other drugs mimic the neurotransmitters. Ultimately, wrong messages are being sent and the person loses their ability to make coherent decisions. This is also true for those who use pornography, gambling, or food as their drug of choice. When the drug of choice is being used, neurotransmitters such as dopamine are transmitted across the neurons at a higher rate than normal, thus changing and creating new neural pathways. I will explain more about this later.

Okay, you say, *but what does this have to do with actually being addicted?* Let me explain further. There is a part of your brain called the reptilian brain. This is also called the VTA or the ventral regimental area. It is located in the central part of your brain. I like the term reptilian because it reminds me of how reptiles act. If you think about it, reptiles are always ready for fight, flight, or freeze. (I will come back to these terms later.) But for now, these are instinct terms. When you are in your mom's belly, this is the part of your brain that forms first because it helps regulate the beating of your heart. It is part of the sympathetic nervous system. This system is what keeps you more alert and hyper vigilant. It lets you know if you are in danger, so you know how to protect yourself. Yes, this is also the anxiety producing part of your brain, but this part of the brain makes sure all of your human needs are being satisfied, such as hunger, protecting yourself from the cold, getting enough sleep, etc. This part of the brain contains the amygdala as well. The amygdala takes in all the sights, sounds, and smells (you know, sensory information) and processes it to make sure you are safe. We will learn more about the amygdala later in another chapter when talking about PTSD–post-traumatic stress disorder. Overall, the reptilian part of your brain says, *I've got to survive, so I better be prepared.*

The next part of the brain we must discuss is the nucleus accumbens. This is located closer to the front of the brain and higher than the reptilian part of the brain. This is where the basal ganglia "hangs" out. The basal ganglia take part in pleasures such as eating, sex, and connection with others. This is the pleasure center or reward center of your brain. It is actually a really great part of the brain, I think. I mean, who doesn't want pleasure right? When we do something we enjoy such as eating chocolate covered mint Oreos—oh yes, that's a favorite of mine—dopamine neurons travel from the reptilian part of the brain over to the nucleus accumbens. If you don't know what dopamine is, it's a wonderful chemical that makes you feel good and helps you to focus on what you are doing. Dopamine is a neurotransmitter that helps us decide between what is pleasurable and what is not. Side note: People with ADD or ADHD do not get enough dopamine and therefore, it is hard for them to focus unless it's something really interesting.

Another major part of the brain that is important to understand is the pre-frontal cortex. This is the front part of your brain that takes a huge role in logical reasoning. It is also called the executive functioning part of the brain. This is where you make all your logical decisions. Now I don't want to single anyone out, but have you noticed that girls mature faster than boys both physically and mentally? That is because girls' pre-frontal cortexes mature much faster than boys. Girls' pre-frontal cortexes fully mature between the ages of 23-26 years old, but boys don't fully mature until 26-30 years old. Can you imagine using drugs or drinking at such a young age that your brain is still trying to develop? I have had clients who have come to get treatment for their addiction and have talked about using at the young age of four years old. I know that this is not scientific, but I can see a small difference in how they talk and behave versus those who used much later in life. Scientifically speaking, research has shown that using at such a young age does affect the brain in negative way (Winters & Arria, 2011). The good news is that the brain can heal over time with sobriety.

The reptilian brain, nucleus accumbens, and the pre-frontal cortex work together to decide what you need, how it feels, and if it is logical. Unfortunately, feelings and logic don't always agree. Let me explain how addiction works in these parts of the brain. For instance, a person chooses to use cocaine for the first time. The cocaine enters the body and makes its way to the brain. The neurons in the reptilian part of the brain are being overridden by the cocaine particles. Instead of the neurotransmitters connecting to the receptors, cocaine mimics the neurotransmitters and makes its own connection to the receptors. The neurons connect with the nucleus accumbens or basal ganglia and tell it to produce dopamine. When a person uses cocaine, the dopamine levels are much higher than usual. Dopamine does more than make you feel good, it helps your brain to be able to remember pleasurable experiences. Dopamine tells the brain that this feels good and then as the cocaine continues to mimic the neurotransmitters, it ultimately "shuts off" the pre-frontal cortex; thereby losing the logical thinking in the brain. If a person continues to use cocaine, the reptilian brain recognizes it as something it *needs* in order to survive. This is because the nucleus accumbens is telling the reptilian brain that this feels good, and this good feeling is needed; not just wanted. The substance helps to numb out the bad feelings such as emotions or sometimes physical feelings. Your survival brain is saying, *Yeah, this is good, this means we are safe from all the bad stuff! We need this to survive!* And now we are addicted because in part, it helps us to numb all the bad feelings. Unfortunately, it also numbs all the good feelings too. Overall, the reptilian and the nucleus accumbens get together and collaborate to get you to take the easy way out. Easy for the brain, but not for you.

Ultimately, you have now created new neural pathways in your brain that specifically tell you it's time to use and/or drink. Look at it this way, you know that water will *always* take the pathway of least resistance. This is like the neural pathways in the brain that develop with your drug or alcohol use. Every time you feel angry, sad, embarrassed, etc., your brain wants you to automatically reach for your drug to make you feel better or rather numb the pain. Sometimes you don't realize what you're doing when you say, *I am not going to drink today,* and then you find yourself in the liquor store buying a fifth. Your brain becomes automatic. We all do this. No one thinks about getting ready in the morning. You don't have to think about buttoning your buttons or tying your shoes. You automatically know how to do those things because you've created neural pathways and muscle memory to help you do it without having to think about it. Likewise, it is the same thing that happens when you drink or use; it becomes automatic.

Have you ever used a password for a long time and then the website tells you that you must change it? You change the password and then the next time you go to the website, you type in the old password. It takes you a few times to remember to type in the new password, but it is kind of irritating because you have to be more vigilant in your thinking. In committing to memory the new password, you are creating a new neural pathway. The old pathway is still there, but now you have bypassed it and are using the new path that has been created. This is what you will learn how to do in later chapters—create new neural pathways to help overcome your addiction.

This is the basics of addiction, which I like to call the Science of Addiction 101. If you would like more information, you can research *How Addiction Affects the Brain.* This will bring up several websites that will give you a more in depth understanding on how addiction works in the brain.

CHAPTER 3
ADDICTION AFFECTS OUR SPIRIT

I cannot talk about the physical aspect of addiction and not talk about how addiction affects the spirit. In Romans 8:16 it reads, "The Spirit itself beareth witness with our spirit, that we are the children of God." What I take from this is that God's Holy Spirit can speak to us and tell us some pretty amazing truths. Likewise, the adversary is a spirit and so are his followers, and they have the potential to tempt us into making bad choices as well as tell us some pretty amazing lies and half-truths.

Every child is born with the Light of Christ (John1:9). We all have this light within us, and as we yield "to the enticings of the Holy Spirit," we will increase "in wisdom and stature, and in favour with God and man" (Mosiah 3:19 & Luke 2:52). This tells me that as we listen to the Holy Spirit, God will teach us and help us to learn and grow spiritually. This also tells me our light will grow and shine as well. When we yield to the "enticings" of the adversary, then obviously our light grows dark. This scripture illustrates it perfectly: "O, my beloved brethren, remember the awfulness in transgressing against that Holy God, and also the awfulness of yielding to the enticings of that cunning one. Remember, to be carnally-minded is death, and to be spiritually minded is life eternal" (2 Nephi 9:39). If you read this scripture and think, *Oh great, thanks for reminding me about how awful I feel about my own addiction and "following Satan,"* I hope you realize this is not the case, because there is always hope. This was not meant to bring up any negative thoughts but rather the understanding that the adversary plays a great role in helping to keep us addicted.

The adversary does not want you to be happy. You have heard the saying *misery loves company?* The adversary is so miserable, he wants you to be miserable with him. This is his great mission in life. How come? Because he is jealous of our eternal progression. In heaven, we chose not to follow Satan. We chose to come to earth to receive physical bodies because we knew this was important for us to be able to progress and to eventually become perfect. Yes, I said it, *Perfect.* You already know that we will never become perfect in this life, but this life is for us to practice and learn how to become perfect. Remember what Brad Wilcox said in one of his books, "[w]e are learning heaven" (Wilcox, 2013, p.16). If we choose to follow the Savior, we will have eternal life. If we choose to follow the cunning one, we will have spiritual death. It sounds so simple, and yet so difficult because the adversary is just that–cunning. Why not—he's had hundreds of years to perfect his cunningness to help make us miserable. It is now our job to listen and discern what is from the devil and what is from the Lord.

I remember one time feeling really sorry for myself. I had been struggling with my family's financial situation for almost fifteen years. My husband was living with his parents and our two older children. I took the four younger children to live with me at my dad's cabin about two hours away. I was so angry and frustrated. I was allowing the negative thoughts and feelings to overcome my mental and physical well-being. I remember standing in front of the mirror fixing my hair and this thought came to me: *See, the Lord doesn't care about you.* Holy cow! I knew this thought was not my own and was from the adversary. The feelings that came along with this thought were confusion and anger. I know that Satan is the author of confusion (1 Corinthians 14:33), and I knew I needed to get on my knees and pray.

The point I am trying to make is that we get whisperings from the Spirit and we get whisperings from the adversary. The more we choose to discern and listen to the whisperings from the Spirit, the more our light grows within our own spirit and the closer we become to God. The more we choose to listen to the whisperings from the adversary, the more the light within our spirit darkens. We become farther from God. We are either progressing or digressing; there is no sitting on the fence.

The more we partake in our addiction, the more our spirit darkens, and we lose communion with God. We are then more susceptible to the enticings of the adversary. Shame is from the adversary. He wants us to feel shameful. We mask over that shame with addiction or deflect it with lies to ourselves that also come from the adversary. Lies such as: *See, the Lord doesn't care about you.* I am going to talk more about this in another chapter.

One last thing I want to share in this chapter is the conflict we have between what we know to be true and how we feel about ourselves and our behaviors. As members of the church, we strive to keep the commandments because we love Jesus and because He has asked us to keep them. With Satan and the natural man or our brain working against us, we will always fall short. Then we hear the words, *I'm not good enough. I'm not smart enough. I'm not worthy of love. See, the Lord doesn't care about me.* These thoughts are from Satan. Period. But because our feelings come so strongly with the thought, we feel like they are our own thoughts. We feel like they become our "truth." This reinforces a negative core belief inside of us, and weakens our resolve to follow our light.

There you have it. You now know how the brain works when it comes to addiction, and you know that the adversary and your brain work against you to make the right decisions, sometimes. The good news is that there are ways to "putteth off the natural man" and break free from the shame that binds you (Mosiah 3:19).

Chapter 4

Mental Illness and Addiction

I once had a client who came in for counseling, but not because she wanted counseling. In order for her to get medication, she had to come in for counseling once a month. She had been diagnosed with Borderline Personality Disorder (American Psychiatric Association, 2017). In my practice, I have met several people with this disorder, and in general it stems from severe childhood trauma. This woman had severe trauma, and I really felt bad for her, but she would not do the homework I gave her. All she wanted were the pills that were prescribed for her anxiety. I'll admit I was frustrated with her and told her flat out, "You don't want to do any of the homework I give you, and you call up asking to get more medication before your prescription is expired. People will think you are addicted unless you follow what the experts ask of you." I knew she was addicted, but I had no proof. She got terribly upset with me that I would accuse her of being an addict and left. I felt bad about the situation, and even though it was true, I probably could have handled it better due to her mental illness.

I mention this story because mental illness with addiction (comorbidity) is highly prevalent in our culture. You might have a mental illness and not even know it, or maybe you already know you have a mental illness. Either way, it is important to see an expert to get the help you need.

I do not personally like mental diagnosis as it sometimes puts a label on people and perpetuates the negative stigma around mental illness. The truth is that unless we figure out what is not working for us, we can't make it better. Most of my clients have either anxiety or depression or both. Generally, if you have anxiety, you will have depression too, but not always. For some reason, depression and anxiety like living together, however, if you have depression, you do not necessarily always have anxiety. For those who have anxiety, you are familiar with the constant pressure or angst in your chest that doesn't seem to go away. Maybe you have depression where the foreboding sense of sadness looms constantly. These "illnesses" can be quite debilitating and frankly, the stigma of anxiety and depression has not improved much in our culture. Although, the past couple of decades can be seen with optimism as people try to help others understand mental illness.

Many of my clients have used alcohol, drugs, and other addictions to help themselves feel normal. I had a client who was diagnosed with Bipolar Disorder. You may have heard people say "She must be bipolar," even when she is not. The Bipolar Disorder diagnoses is given to those who become manic and then severely depressed and then back to manic again and so on. You can read more about it in the Diagnostic and Statistical Manual of Mental disorders, also known as the DSM-5-TR (American Psychiatric Association, 2022). Without proper medication, which can take a while to perfect, people with Bipolar Disorder can be mentally unstable and do ridiculous things. When in her manic state, my client had the need to act out sexually. When in her depressive state, she would lie in bed all day. At first, she didn't why she was acting out, and reported that when she used heroin. The heroin helped her feel normal. Many times, because of their mental illness, people will use alcohol and drugs to feel normal. In fact, many people with ADHD will use prescription methamphetamines to help them concentrate. The point is that a person needs to either find the right medication to help them control their mental illness without becoming addicted, or learn skills and tools to help them manage their mental state.

I want to share with you a few mental health disorders that may or may not be prevalent in your life. Therefore, by understanding these disorders, you can learn to recognize them within your won life and possibly within the lives of those you love. Once identified, you can begin to understand how addiction plays a role in mental health issues and consequently take the necessary actions to get the help you or your loved one needs.

Interestingly enough, anxiety is the top mental health issue I see in my practice. Anxiety affects everyone at some point in their life. For some, it can be debilitating, and for others, it's their constant daily companion. Many don't realize they have anxiety because they believe it's natural to feel that way on a daily basis. Even though anxiety is good for us, to a degree, it can cause serious issues long-term. Some of these issues include irritable bowel syndrome, chronic digestion, etc. Why can it be so good for us? Anxiety helps us to stay alert and motivated to get things done. However, the effects of anxiety don't feel good. Many experience excessive worry, irritability, restlessness, low energy, and sleep disturbance. What's worse is the constant pressure in your chest that won't go away. It almost feels like you're having a heart attack, which at times can turn into a panic attack.

Depression happens to be the second top mental health issue I see in my practice. Depression presents itself in many forms, such as feeling sad and depressed nearly every day, diminished interest in hobbies or activities, increased or decreased appetite, loss of energy, feelings of worthlessness and hopelessness, being unable to concentrate, and thoughts of suicide. You don't have to have all of these symptoms to be depressed, however, these are many of the symptoms that coincide with depression. This mental health issue hinders our well-being far beyond description. It's understandable why many choose to use alcohol and drugs to numb the pain of depression. This dark chasm of hopelessness is one of the hardest mental health issues to overcome.

Bipolar disorder is often misunderstood. As described above, many will use this term loosely to portray a person who easily maneuvers their way from one extreme to another. Obviously, this is not always the case. There are two main types of bipolar disorder—I and II. For our purposes, I will give the general description. People who are diagnosed with bipolar disorder generally work through manic and depressive cycles. When they are manic, they might experience inflated self-esteem, decreased need for sleep, are easily distracted, more talkative, increased goal-directed activities, and may engage in maladaptive behaviors. When a person is in their depressive state, they will experience all of the depressive symptoms such as increased or decreased appetite, loss of energy, feelings of worthlessness and hopelessness, being unable to concentrate, etc. These episodes can last for weeks or months at a time, depending on your bipolar type. What makes this mental health issue so difficult is dealing with the constant extremes.

It's unfortunate that narcissistic personality disorder is becoming more common nowadays, or at least it appears to be more prevalent in our culture. I mention this mental disorder because we all know someone who has this disorder or is affected by this disorder in some way. You may also recognize that the person with narcissistic personality disorder has some type of addiction. Do you recall in Greek mythology the striking character Narcissus? He fell in love with a reflection of himself and felt that no one was good enough for him except for himself. In this type of personality disorder, the person generally cares only for themselves. People with this disorder may have a grandiose sense of self-importance, believe they are better than others, have a strong sense of entitlement, will take advantage of others, can be arrogant, etc. They are also exceptionally good at masking over their emotions and feelings. People with narcissistic personality disorder will use all types of abuse to show their importance or to achieve their means.

Another debilitating diagnosis, which many of us have or have had, is Post-Traumatic Stress Disorder, more commonly known as PTSD. Those who experience PTSD symptoms such as panic attacks, memory loss, flashbacks, anxiety, nightmares, depression, feelings of detachment, and exaggerated negative beliefs. These symptoms can last for years.

Bear with me as I veer off the subject a moment because I want to explain why our bodies have these symptoms when we have experienced chronic or accute trauma. I call it: How Trauma Affects the Brain 101. If you recall from the chapter on how the brain works with addiction, you may remember a part of your brain called the amygdala. This part of your brain takes in all the sights, sounds, smells, and what you can physically feel. It basically takes in all the sensory information that surrounds you and tells your reptilian brain that you are safe. No cause for alarm. You can continue your day as planned and you do not need to worry.

You have another part of your brain called the hippocampus. This part is amygdala's friend and tells the amygdala that it's okay to process or download the information it's receiving to the higher functioning parts of the brain. Amygdala sends the information to the higher functioning parts of the brain, and it's all processed and good. Then danger strikes. Maybe you got in a car accident, or maybe you were yelled at by your boss. Maybe it was trauma that has lasted over a significant amount of time such as your parent constantly yelling at you when you were younger. It can be anything that goes against your core belief system that tells your brain it is not safe.

Your amygdala takes in all the information from this trauma and the hippocampus, says *Hey amygdala, let's process this information into the higher functioning parts of the brain.* Amygdala says, *No way! Are you crazy? I can't let go of this information. This is serious stuff! We are not safe. I need to make sure I hold on to this information so that we can be prepared for the next time this happens!* Amygdala does not let the information process, but rather keeps it stored so the next time something happens it will be prepared. What does "prepared" really mean? In this case, prepared means our brains will go into fight, flight, or freeze mode, also known as the sympathetic system. Whenever we have a sight, sound, smell, or anything that is remotely similar to our trauma, the amygdala gets hijacked and alerts our sympathetic system to do something. Many times, it is in the form of a flashback. Sometimes it is memory loss. In this case we may fight by getting angry and yelling, or we may do our best to get away from the situation because we feel our anxiety getting stronger. A lot of times we might have a downright panic attack. The sympathetic system also sends signals to the pre-frontal cortex to "shut off." This cuts off the logical part of your brain. Even though you aren't going to die from a panic attack, your body reacts as though you are going to die. People experiencing panic attacks feel the stress of life-or-death situations. The reptilian part of the brain says, *I'm in control right now, so you need to stay in the back seat. There is no logic needed here because we have to survive!*

There is a great book that addresses PTSD called The Body Keeps the Score, by Dr. Bessel van der Kolk (2015). He shares a lot of information on how to address PTSD from EMDR to yoga. For your information, EMDR is Eye Movement Desensitization Reprocessing. This technique helps a person to process their trauma into the higher functioning parts of the brain. It is done through bilateral processing which can include the eyes moving back and forth while viewing a light, or buzzers buzzing in the person's hands back and forth. This technique has proven to be highly effective in helping people reduce their symptoms of PTSD. In fact, "as many as 90% of trauma survivors appeared to have no PTSD symptoms after just three sessions" (Leonard, 2019).

There are of course many other mental health disorders within our society. I mention these top five because they are the most frequent among the population. It's important to understand that many people who suffer from mental illness also suffer from an addiction. Using alcohol or other drugs is a way for people to numb their pain, and to feel somewhat normal. The good news is you can overcome addiction, but it is going to take work, perseverance, and building a strong relationship with our Savior. It's possible you have tried many times to quit your addiction already, but mental illness may be holding you back from your success. I want to add a small point that can make a huge difference in your life. I don't believe in taking drugs and alcohol to feel normal or to numb the pain, but I do believe in working towards finding the right medication that can ease your burdens. Taking prescribed medication by a professional in its proper amount can help you work towards the freedom you desire. Be smart about it as you thoroughly look into professional help. I also recommend mental health professionals who can give you more skills and tools to fight your addiction. This is now your time to break free from your shame with the help of professionals and the Savior. You can do this, so reclaim your life!

Chapter 5

Physical Health vs Mental Health in Addiction

I had a client who had been morbidly obese for most of his life. He lost a good amount of weight, married for a time, had a daughter, and eventually divorced. He turned back to his food addiction after his divorce and gained the weight back. His physical health was affecting his mental health. He came to counseling because of his depression. It turns out his depression was due to his obesity. Of course, you do not have to be obese to be depressed. What we do with our bodies can affect our mental state so much that we can become mentally ill.

When it comes to our mental health, we need to take care of our physical health as well. It is difficult being human and having to deal with the constant battle between the spiritual mind and the carnal mind. The spiritual mind is your personality, the real you. The carnal mind refers to our natural desires such as desires for food, sex, and connection. If not kept in check, these natural desires can cause serious issues in our lives. It is the "natural man who is the enemy to God" (Mosiah 3:19). There is a battle that occurs between these two, and, unfortunately, the carnal mind wins a lot of the time.

The carnal mind tends to take control of our actions when we do not take care of our physical health and well-being. Have you ever gotten angry because you need your next "fix?" You might not be an angry person, but you lashed out because of your physical turmoil. My husband understands

25

very well that I get angry when I am hungry. I get hangry, a lot. If I start to lash out at him, he will try to get me some food because he knows I can be a hangry person.

When we do not take care of our bodies, it affects our mental health and can cause mental illness. In 2008, I attempted to transplant a tree in my backyard. It was located in an odd spot, and I felt that it needed to have a new home in the farthest corner of my backyard. I picked it up, and quickly carried it to its new spot. It weighed over 100 pounds! Unfortunately, I injured my lower back. I thought I had dealt with it by going to the chiropractor and allowing it to heal, but eight years later it came back to bite me. I developed arthritis in my lower back, plus I had extreme sciatic pain to where I could barely walk. I lost the ability to walk normally and was not able to perform tasks as well as I used to. I went to the doctor and he gave me Ibuprofen. That was not helpful. I did not want to take Ibuprofen for the rest of my life. I went to the chiropractor but that only helped a little bit. Pretty soon depression hit, and I was able to do very little around the house. I could barely take care of my kids. I was at my wits end and pleading with the Lord for help.

This back issue lasted for about five months. I know many of you have health issues that have lasted for years, and I don't want this to discredit what you have been through, but for me at that time, five months felt like five years. I began to research on the internet (boy, I love the internet) and found some solutions that I tried. It turns out that I had a muscle that was spasming in my back right near my sciatica nerve. When it spasmed, it would put pressure on the sciatic nerve and cause a lot of pain. I found that huge doses of vitamin C and some magnesium were the key to healing my pain. I then used multivitamins to help with my arthritis. I am not saying this will cure you if you have any types of pain in your body. If you do, I encourage you to do your research and see a specialist if needed. I am saying how this small example of taking good care of my body also helped in taking good care of my mental health. My depression was difficult to handle during those months, but as soon as I took care of my physical well-being, my depression subsided. What I'd like you to understand is that our mental health is affected by our physical well-being, at least to a degree. If we take care of the physical, we have a better chance of improving our mental state.

Have you ever heard of fecal matter transplant? It is where they take some of the "poo" from a healthy person and transplant it into the intestine of the unhealthy person. Apparently, the gut is our second "brain." If we do not have a healthy gut, then that can cause a lot of mental health issues. I have had two clients who have had this transplant. One of my clients was extremely autistic. His mother told me that he could barely talk and would never look at people. After his transplant, my client (her son) was able to talk to people and look them in the eye. I was suprised that he was able to communicate with me directly, as well as amazed that the treatment helped his well-being. I share this with you to help you understand that our bodies are complicated. We need to be aware of the many ways we can help our mental health. One avenue of treatment may work for some, and other avenues of treatment can work for others. The point is that by taking care of our physical bodies—eating healthy and taking vitamins—we can deter many diseases and mental health issues. This includes taking care of our gut. I cannot recommend vitamins and *lots* of vegetables enough! Make sure your body is getting the recommended intake of vitamins (not the cheap ones) and minerals. It is possible that having the right amount of nutrients can help you fight cravings and urges. I had a woman once tell me about her brother who was fighting alcoholism. She said that once he started taking the vitamins she gave him, he did not crave alcohol anymore, at least not nearly as much as he used to. I know that as you work on getting your proper nutrition, this will help with so many issues, both physically and mentally.

I also need to share with you some information about exercising. Dr. Daniel Amen, a psychiatrist who studies the brain and uses brain scans to look at how the brain is functioning, says in his Book, *Change Your Brain, Change Your Life,* that cardiovascular exercise is more for your brain that it is for your body. Aerobic exercise is so good for your brain. In fact, Dr. Amen says, "Exercise can also be very helpful in calming worries and increasing cognitive flexibility" (Amen,1998, p.185). He also says ". . . exercise increases your energy levels and may distract you from the bad thoughts that tend to loop" (p.185). He says that most psychiatrists do not even look at the organ they are treating. Dr. Amen wanted to be able to look at the organ he treats, so he created the SPECT scan. He has been able to show how exercise, especially cardiovascular exercise helps improve our mental health. If you are not already exercising, then I encourage you to get in at least one and a half hours of cardio a week. Also, you might be interested in Dr. Amens book, *Change Your Brain, Change Your Life* as he shares foods and remedies you can use and do to help your mental health.

Lastly, aside from eating well and exercising, I want to mention sleep. Sleep is so good for your mental health. If you are a parent, you understand the importance of sleep. When those newborn babies are brought home, they take all of your good sleep away, and before you know it, you lash out at people, or you can't remember what you wanted to say. You almost feel as if you are going crazy! The lack of sleep does this to us, and although we are busy people, we tend to get only 5-6 hours of sleep a night! Please work on getting your 7-8 hours of sleep a night as this will improve your mental health. If you need medication, then do it. Good sleep can change your life!

If you are not eating right, exercising, or getting good sleep, it can cause physical and mental issues. I hope you will take this into account as you work on breaking free from your shame. In order for us to break free from our shame of addiction, we need to keep ourselves mentally healthy, and it starts with taking care of ourselves physically.

CHAPTER 6

THE POWER OF SHAME

There is something in our minds that judges everybody and everything, including the weather, the dog, the cat - everything. The inner Judge uses what is in our Book of Law to judge everything we do and don't do, everything we think and don't think, and everything we feel and don't feel. Everything lives under the tyranny of this Judge. Every time we do something that goes against the Book of Law, the Judge says we are guilty, we need to be punished, we should be ashamed. This happens many times a day, day after day, for all the years of our lives (Ruiz, 1997, p.9).

I love the book *The Four Agreements* by Don Miguel Ruiz. Dr. Ruiz writes about shame in unique ways, thus the paragraph above. He also shared in his book how animals will make a mistake, think of it once, learn from it, and then move on. The animals don't ruminate or continue to think about their mistake like humans do. Humans will make a mistake and then ruminate about it and beat themselves up over their mistake. Not only do humans beat themselves up, but they will continue to beat themselves up repeatedly. When will we learn to be more kind and gentler to ourselves? When will we be able to learn from our mistakes and move on?

I am going to say it again: Shame is of the devil! It is that feeling that makes you want to crawl into a hole and use, and/or die. It tells you that you are not worthy of love and belonging. It breeds disconnection. It breeds fear. Shame is a worthless feeling that brings nothing but heartache and misery, and a lot of it is due to the belief, *I am not worthy of love and belonging. I am not worthy of connection.* Let me share with you some of the shameful things my clients have shared with me:

I feel shame that my addiction has taken so much lost quality time away from my wife and kids.

I feel that I am not worthy of my family's love and support. I feel I let them down.

I've done cocaine, Xanax, acid, and pot when I should have been taking care of my kid.

I feel shame that my roommate could quit drinking without help, and I couldn't.

I feel shame that my drinking has pushed friends away.

I get lost in my thoughts and I act like everything is okay when it's not and I don't share it with anyone.

I got into a car accident drunk. I've lost touch with family. I've attempted suicide, and have ruined relationships because of my addiction.

Shame perpetuates my addiction because I feel like I'm a "mess up," then I use that as a way to rationalize continuing to make poor choices.

I've gotten four DUIs in the last 10 years.

My shame causes me to feel like I'm completely worthless and I deserve nothing.

I feel shame about my loss of ambition, self-confidence, and self-esteem.

I'm shameful for stealing to obtain drugs.

My daughters weren't allowed to be alone with me because of my addiction, then I couldn't see them at all because I continued to use.

I have become anti-social.

My family suffers because of my addiction.

My parents have had to help me out financially due to my addiction.

I am so full of shame for my behavior and my drinking, I have totally humiliated myself and to numb the pain, I drink and that makes the pain worse.

I am sure you can at least relate to one of these shameful feelings. You can see how shame can be so severe and helps keep you in your addiction. How do we break free from the shame of addiction? Aren't you tired of beating yourself up over your drug use? Don't you want the freedom when being wholehearted?

In her book, Dr. Brown talks about being wholehearted, and if you are to be a wholehearted person you need to understand what wholeheartedness living is:

> Wholehearted living is about engaging in our lives from a place of worthiness. It means cultivating the courage, compassion, and connection to wake up in the morning and think, *No matter what gets done and how much is left undone, I am enough.* It's going to bed at night thinking, *Yes, I am imperfect and vulnerable and sometimes afraid, but that doesn't change the truth that I am also brave and worthy of love and belonging* (Brown, 2012, p.10).

In other words, wholehearted living is about giving ourselves unconditional compassion, which consequently leads to vulnerability and living life to its fullest. Dr. Brown describes the main difference of a wholehearted person and one who lacks wholeheartedness. She writes, "Those who feel lovable, who love, and who experience belonging simply believe they are *worthy* of love and belonging" (Brown, 2012, p.11). Did you catch the one-word difference? It's the word believe! There are at least five hundred seventy-three variations of the word believe found in the standard works. One of my favorite scriptures is found in Mark 9:23, "Jesus said unto him, If thou canst believe, all things are possible to him that believeth." Belief is powerful!

Core beliefs are beliefs you have formulated over your life span. Dr. Ruiz calls them agreements. These are agreements you have made with yourself. For example, you were told as a child by a trusted adult that you were stupid. Of course, you have already agreed with yourself that this adult is worthy of your trust. You believe or make an agreement with yourself that you must be stupid. Have you ever heard the saying "You are what you believe?" Now you have this core belief that you are stupid, and when someone says to you that you are smart, you don't believe them because you already "know" you're stupid. You will continue to reinforce this belief until it becomes strong. Then it is carried with you throughout your whole life and affects the choices you make and how you behave. Who knows, you may have been destined to be a nuclear physicist, but just didn't think you were smart enough!

There are many core beliefs/agreements we make with ourselves that are maladaptive to our well-being. Starting to recognize those core beliefs and changing them to more adaptive beliefs is the key to breaking free from our shame. As Dr. Brown calls it— *building shame resilience* (2010). There are several ways to build shame resilience and I hope you will work on each concept I share with you in this book because, "[w]holehearted living is not a onetime choice. It is a process" (Brown, 2010, p.1). I do not want you to feel overwhelmed. I want you to take it little by little and practice the concepts, whether it is for the day or the month, I want you to *gradually* work on each concept.

One of these concepts entails *Sharpening Your Sword.* Have you ever heard Steven Covey's *Sharpen the Saw?* This is from his book, *The 7 Habits of Highly Effective People* (Covey, 2013). Sharpen the saw is about taking the time to care for yourself. I call it sharpening your sword. Why? Because some days, life's a battle. To sharpen your sword, you need to take care of yourself: mentally, emotionally, spiritually, and physically every day (Covey, 2013). This is similar to the children and youth programs in the Church, where children and youth make spiritual, social, physical, and intellectual goals. Either way, the point is to take care of yourself daily. For example, I get up, read scriptures, pray, exercise, and eat a healthy breakfast before sending the kids off to school. I listen to self-help books for my mental aspect and make sure to connect emotionally with my husband, kids, and friends (not all on the same day). I have accomplished all four aspects of sharpening my sword so I can be the best wife/mom/friend I can be. Making sure I take care of myself everyday helps keep my sword sharp so when I have my down days, I don't sink deep into despair and turn to my addiction.

Shame in the LDS culture can grow significantly deep because of our understanding of the Gospel of Jesus Christ. We make covenants with our Heavenly Father that are serious. Covenants are two-way promises in that we promise to follow God's commandments, and He promises us spiritual blessings. When we break our promises, we are denied the spiritual blessings. For example, we promise to keep the Word of Wisdom (I will share more about this topic later) and the blessings include better health; physically, mentally, and spiritually. When we break the promise, we may have issues with either our physical, mental, and spiritual health. Sometimes people have issues with all three. Covenants are beautiful promises that we make because we love our Father and His Son. We make covenants because we want to be like the Savior. The blessings we receive from God are like a bonus!

Having an addiction in the LDS culture is one way of breaking our covenants with God. Addiction does not bring us closer to the Savior. Addiction is a terrible monster that controls our lives. In fact, it becomes the master of our souls and bodies, when instead our spirits should be in control. The shame we feel in the LDS culture runs deep because of the expectations of keeping our covenants. Unfortunately, many members of the Church will shame those who have an addiction. This is wrong. Jesus never shamed anyone. Jesus always encouraged, taught, uplifted, and reproved when needed. Yet, when He reproved someone, He always followed it up with love. If you are feeling shamed by those around you, please know they are not following the Savior's way. If you are shaming yourself or others, please know that you are not following the Savior's way. The adversary works extremely hard to make us all feel shame.

The culture in Jesus Christ's church is one of love, understanding, patience, encouragement, long-suffering, charity, hope, faith, etc. I could go on, but what I'm trying to say is that Christ's culture has no shame. I would hope you will never have to feel shame for what you have done. Will you feel sorrow and guilt? Yes, but never shame.

In the next chapters that follow, I am going to talk about different ways to break free from the shame of addiction. These are not miracle cures—well, maybe Jesus' sacrifice for you can be a miracle cure—but with hard work, patience, and the grace you receive both from yourself and from God, you can break free from the binding shackles of shame.

CHAPTER 7

CONNECTION

If you recall from the first chapter, Johann Hari mentioned in his TED Talk, "The opposite of addiction is not sobriety, the opposite of addiction is connection" (2015). Connection is a major catalyst in breaking free from the shame of addiction. I mentioned that connection is why we are here. This is true when it comes to the gospel. In The Church of Jesus Christ of Latter-day Saints, the gospel is centered on the family. Recall the Church's The Family: A Proclamation to the World? Family is central to our eternal lives.

Before we all came to earth, we were all spirits in heaven. There was the Grand Council where God laid out a plan and we chose to either follow the plan or not. Satan and his followers obviously chose not to follow the plan, and he and his followers were cast out of heaven, never to receive a body. We knew that receiving a body was important to God's plan, and we would make a lot of mistakes in our bodies here on earth; a lot of it due to Satan and his followers. We knew the Savior was willing to suffer for our sins and be a sacrifice for us so that we could repent and live with Him again, inheriting have eternal life in new and glorious bodies. What a marvelous plan!

Heavenly Father then put us in families. Why? Because He has His family—us. He understands the importance of connection. Our spirits need connection, and without it, we would be just like the adversary and his followers. Why do think the adversary wants you to feel so much shame? He knows shame breeds disconnection. He knows that loneliness and isolation can pull you down into the depths of despair and may possibly lead to suicide. He's jealous we have bodies, and he doesn't have one because of the decision he made in heaven. He wants us to be miserable just like him.

For a while now, you have had a connection with your drug of choice. You need connection, and sometimes you can't get it from your family and friends due to not feeling worthy of their love and belonging. Maybe you are unsure of how to connect, so, instead, you bond with your drug of choice, and why not? Your drug of choice does not judge you. It's always there for you any time you want it. It has become your best friend. The problem is that your drug of choice does not genuinely care about you like your family and friends do. Yes, family and friends can be judgmental and harsh, but in the long run, they do care and want to connect with you. Your drug of choice can't care. It's a drug. It can only kill you slowly, both physically and/or spiritually. It is there to harm you, but very slowly. I think of using drugs like the frog in the pot. You have a pot of boiling water and you put the frog in. The frog feels the hot temperature and it jumps out quickly. You put the frog in room temperature water and slowly heat it up to boiling and the frog will stay there and die. This is how people with addictions suffer–very slowly. You may not die physically, but you are definitely dying spiritually.

Connection is difficult if you have grown up in a family that lacks good communication skills. Sometimes we learn maladaptive communication skills as defense mechanisms or ways to deflect how we are feeling. There are different types of communication skills such as passive communication, aggressive communication, passive-aggressive communication, and assertive communication.

If you are a passive communicator, you usually don't like conflict and will try to please everyone. You will let things "slide" just to keep the peace. You don't want to cause problems with anyone as you want to keep everyone happy. The problem with passiveness is that over time you will build up a lot of resentment, towards others and yourself, because your needs don't get met. Over time, this resentment builds up and eventually you "explode." You will get angry and lash out at others and possibly yourself. After the "explosion" you feel guilty and ashamed for your behavior because you just want others to be happy. Passive communication is not all bad though. It is good to want to be the peacemaker and to help others out when you can. It is bad when it builds resentment. When this happens, the person needs to take a moment and realize it is happening so they can be more assertive in their communication. I have been a passive communicator for a long time, until I gradually learned more adaptive ways to communicate. I am still working on it though.

If you are an aggressive communicator, you worry more about getting your needs met rather than other people getting their needs met. Aggressive people are just that, aggressive. They will yell, manipulate, and do anything to get their way. They can be quite abusive. The problem with aggressive communication is that aggressive people are usually respected out of fear, not love. They are not liked as well either.

I think passive-aggressiveness is the worst of the maladaptive communication styles. This type of communication style is when one feels a lot of resentment toward others, and instead of telling how they feel, they act as if everything is okay, and then do something to "get back" at the people. Generally, it's in a "sneaky" manner, but not always. The passive-aggressive person is trying to meet the needs of the other person, but they are not getting their own needs met. They become resentful and feel justified in their aggressive behavior because they "helped" the person out. The problem with passive-aggressive communication is that people who are vindictive and do things behind other people's backs are usually deeply hurt within themselves. They feel the need to get back at others because of their own issues within them. They do not know how to truly love themselves. They use this communication style as a type of defense mechanism.

Now for the most adaptive and best communication style: Assertiveness. Assertive people are the best kind. They try to meet the needs of others as well as try to get their own needs met. Assertive people are usually upfront about their intentions. They are kind, understanding, and know when to set boundaries for themselves and others. Assertive people usually have good eye contact, good body language and present themselves confidently. They are sure of themselves and work hard to help others in need. This is the communication style that we all strive for because it is adaptive and helps us to communicate better with our loved ones. Better communication can build stronger relationships which helps aid us in our sobriety.

I hope you are thinking about what type of communication style you use most frequently. Many of us use different communication styles in different settings. I know I'm more passive and assertive at work and can be more aggressive and passive at home. The key to connecting with others is how we treat each other. When we are dealing with things inside of us, maybe an addiction to pornography, the shame we feel makes us believe we are not worthy of love and connection. As a result, often times, our communication breaks down. When others try to connect with us, we put on our defense mechanisms and communicate back in maladaptive ways because subconsciously we feel unworthy of their connection. We start pushing them away. Wow! It seems kind of counter-intuitive, doesn't it? Humans are complicated beings sometimes!

I hope you will take the quiz supplied in the workbook I've developed to find out your communication style. My workbook coincides with this book, and many of the skills and tools shared in this book can be practiced by using the workbook. This PDF workbook can be downloaded for free at http://www.lovenlifebyamanda.org/about-3. The quiz supplied in the workbook is similar to another quiz you can take at: https://amycastro. com/wp-content/uploads/2017/09/Communication-Style-Quiz.pdf. It is a PDF and you can print it off if you'd like. I like this quiz as it gives more detailed information on each communication style. It is not scientific, but it gives you a good indication of what you have as your communication type. Knowing which way you communicate will help you to be mindful of when you are communicating in a maladaptive manner. This will help you to work on being more assertive in your communication.

Connection is not difficult if we follow the Savior. There are many attributes the Savior has that we can learn to acquire. Some of these attributes include compassion, charity, integrity, patience, long-suffering, loyalty, forgiveness, mercy, tenderness, assertiveness, boundary setting, understanding, etc. I could go on, but I think you get the gist. These attributes make real and true connection possible. As you may know, there is a negative side to connection. If these attributes are not followed properly, the adversary can manipulate true connection into false connection. He can make it appear that you are connected when you're really not. If you find that you are or someone you live with is abusive in any way, verbally, physically, sexually, manipulative, gaslighting, deceitful, shaming, etc., then I recommend that you get some professional help. Abusive relationships are not to be taken lightly. They are profoundly serious and can mess with your mental and physical states in extremely negative ways. The more you learn about assertive communication and practice the attributes of the Savior, the more you will begin to see abuse within abusive relationships. It's then your choice to do something about it. Please get professional help if this is the case. Finding support can help you break free from bad relationships. Good connection is incredibly difficult to achieve within bad relationships, and worse, bad relationships can negatively impact other relationships where you might normally find the connection you need.

Some of you might be familiar with Dr. John Gottman. Dr. Gottman studies relationships, specifically couples. Dr. Gottman and his colleagues conducted a study in the mid-1980's where they developed what was called, *The Love Lab* (Love Lab, 2019). Dr. Gottman and his colleagues took an average apartment and put cameras up in the living room and kitchen. Gottman and his colleagues then asked couples to come and stay in the apartment for the weekend (one couple at a time of course) and act how they usually act with each other. Gottman and his colleagues noticed how the couples would do what Gottman calls "placing bids." A bid is a way to connect with other people. For example: A husband and wife are walking down the street and the husband says, "Woah! Look at this Shelby GT 500 Mustang! It's got the cool spoiler and look at those rims! I love the color with the two black stripes down the middle! This car is amazing!" Hubby is placing a bid as he relays all these "cool" things about the car. He's really saying subconsciously, *Honey, I love you so much, and I want to build a connection with you. I'm really enjoying this moment, and I want to connect with you, by you enjoying this moment with me.* Now the wife has a choice to make. She can "turn towards the bid" and connect with her husband and say, *Wow honey, that's a great looking car. I love the rims. I think the black stripes make the car stand out.* Or wifey can "turn away from the bid" and say, *Yeah, that's nice. Listen, we have dinner with the Jones' at 5 pm tonight. We better get going.* If she turns toward the bid, then hubby will feel a stronger connection with wifey. He will feel validated and loved. If wifey turns away from the bid, hubby may not get mad, but subconsciously he will feel shaded, and ultimately feel unloved. If wifey continues to turn away from the bid, then over time their connection will fall apart.

In Gottman's research he called the couples who stayed together the Masters, and those who ended up splitting he called the Disasters. Gottman found that the Masters turned toward the bids 87% of the time, where the Disasters turned toward the bids only 33% of the time (Smith, 2020). Gottman wanted to know what it was that made the Masters more fruitful. He and his colleagues discovered there were two basic traits the Masters had more of than the Disasters. These two basic traits are: Kindness and Generosity. Why? For starters, kindness and generosity are not the same thing. Think about it, you can be kind, but not generous. You can be generous, but not kind. To be a Master, you must have both. For example: You come home from a long day of work and you are really tired. Your loved one comes up to you to tell you about their day. They are placing a bid. You are so tired that you just do not have the energy to accept the bid. You have three choices you can make. You can turn away from the bid and say, *Can you leave me alone please? I'm tired.* Or you can turn towards the bid and be generous with your energy and time and be kind and say, *Yes, tell me about your day. I hope it was a good one.* Or if you do not have the energy at that time you can say, *I'm sorry. I know you want to talk to me, but I need some time to relax. I'm going to go take a shower and when I'm done, I promise to give you my full attention.* This is the assertive technique. Remember, when you are assertive, you work on getting your needs met while also trying to compromise and meet the needs of others.

I hope you can see how true connection takes certain qualities and skills. It is not easy to say the least. I am still learning on how to connect with my daughter who can be overly aggressive. This does not bode well for me who can be very passive. She tends to walk all over me! I am still learning on how to be more assertive and set boundaries with myself and with my daughter.

If you are going to build true connection, you will need to work on becoming more assertive in your communication skills as well as develop Christlike attributes, including kindness and generosity. Remember, Jesus was always kind, but he wasn't always nice. There is a big difference. Jesus knew how to be assertive in his communication and set boundaries. I encourage you to work on Christlike attributes to help improve your connections with others, including turning towards the bids. The stronger the connection, the stronger your sobriety.

CHAPTER 8

THE 12 STEPS

If you have ever been to an Alcohol Anonymous (AA) meeting, you are familiar with their 12 Steps. If you are not familiar, here are the 12 Steps of AA:

- We admitted we were powerless over alcohol-that our lives had become unmanageable.
- Came to believe that a Power greater than ourselves could restore us to sanity.
- Made a decision to turn our will and our lives over to the care of God *as we understood Him.*
- Made a searching and fearless moral inventory of ourselves.
- Admitted to God, to ourselves, and to another human being the exact nature of our wrongs.
- We're entirely ready to have God remove all these defects of character.
- Humbly asked Him to remove our shortcomings.
- Made a list of all persons we had harmed, and became willing to make amends to them all.
- Made direct amends to such people wherever possible, except when to do so would injure them or others.
- Continued to take personal inventory and when we were wrong promptly admitted it.

41

- Sought through prayer and meditation to improve our conscious contact with God *as we understood Him,* praying only for knowledge of His will for us and the power to carry that out.
- Having had a spiritual awakening as the result of these steps, we tried to carry this message to alcoholics, and to practice these principles in all our affairs.

Alcoholics Anonymous World Services Inc., 2016, p.5

I have no doubt that the 12 Steps of AA were inspired of God to be able to help people with an addiction all over the world. The first step of AA is to admit you are powerless over your addiction. Many people with an addiction whom I have spoken to do not like the first step. They tell me, "I'm not powerless. I chose to fall deep into my addiction, and I can choose to get out of it." That may be the case for some, but if you recall from the previous chapter about the neuroscience of addiction, your mind tells you it's time to quit and your brain says, *No way!* It becomes a power struggle. Being powerless over your addiction does not mean you do not have free will and choice. Being powerless means you are a human who makes mistakes because of your powerful addiction within your brain. Plus, you have the adversary tempting you like crazy because he doesn't want to see you succeed! Powerless also means we are submitting ourselves or rather humbling ourselves before God so that He can help perfect us. We cannot perfect ourselves without the enabling power of the Atonement. Alma 34:9 reads, ". . . there must be an atonement made, or else all mankind must unavoidably perish, yea, all are hardened; yea, all are fallen and are lost, and must perish except it be though the atonement which is expedient should be made." This illustrates my point well in that we are all fallen and lost if we do not have and use the Savior's atonement in our lives.

I have had several people share with me that they aren't sure if they believe in a power greater than themselves. If this is the case with you, that's okay. It takes time and patience to develop a relationship with a higher power. I would hope that along with reading this book, you will take the time to read the scriptures and pray. I had a Branch President (kind of like a Bishop) once tell me about his conversion story. He said he never really prayed before because he didn't feel the need to speak to a higher power. The missionaries told him he needed pray. He recalled being in the bathroom or the bedroom and would try to pray but he felt like he was talking to a brick wall. Nevertheless, he persisted in his prayers, and he said over time (it took a while), he felt something change, and he eventually had a strong spiritual experience that helped him believe in God. If you don't feel connected to a higher power, then I encourage you to have patience and perseverance with really wanting a higher power, because if you don't have a desire, then you're not going to find anything. At least having a desire to want a desire is progress. I guarantee that if you don't give up, you will find your own spiritual experience and know that there is a God above who loves you and wants to help you, but He can't help if you don't ask.

The 12 Steps of AA are wonderful steps and, in every sense, have helped thousands of people break free from their addiction. However, the *Addiction Recovery Program: A Guide to Addiction Recovery and Healing* (2005, p.iv) is inspired of God for members of the Church. Some of the steps are similar to the 12 Steps of AA but include inspired scriptures and doctrine which can help an individual grow deeper in their understanding of Christ as well as grow deeper in their relationship with Christ. The Church's 12 Steps are wonderful too, and will help you to find your Higher Power. The Church's 12 Steps include:

- Admit that you, of yourself, are powerless to overcome your addictions and that your life has become unmanageable.
- Come to believe that the power of God can restore you to complete spiritual health.
- Decide to turn your will and your life over to the care of God, the Eternal Father, and His Son, Jesus Christ.
- Make a searching and fearless written moral inventory of yourself.
- Admit to yourself, to your Heavenly Father in the name of Jesus Christ, to proper priesthood authority, and to another person the exact nature of your wrongs.
- Become entirely ready to have God remove all your character weaknesses.
- Humbly ask Heavenly Father to remove your shortcomings.
- Make a written list of all persons you have harmed and become willing to make restitution to them.
- Wherever possible, make direct restitution to all persons you have harmed.
- Continue to take personal inventory, and when you are wrong promptly admit it.

- Seek, through prayer and meditation, to know the Lord's will and to have the power to carry it out.
- Having had a spiritual awakening as a result of the Atonement of Jesus Christ, share this message with others and practice these principles in all you do.

Can you tell the difference between 12 Steps of AA and the Church's 12 Steps? They are similar, but different. I promise that if you take the time, with real intent, to work through the Church's 12 Steps, you will start to see changes. It is a beautiful program that has helped change many hearts and many lives. I encourage you to attend group meetings if you can. Having others with the same needs and desires can be a strong support system in your sobriety.

The Savior understands more about addiction than any of us. He understands our cravings, urges, pains, sorrows, etc. Because of this, the Savior will never shame you or want you to feel shame for your addiction. He loves you because He knows you. He knows you better than you know yourself. Even though you may feel shame now, know that it is possible to overcome it and break free from it, because the Savior has already borne the full weight of your shame and addiction. He knows how to help you through it.

CHAPTER 9

THE SUPERPOWER OF MINDFULNESS

It all begins with . . . Mindfulness. I am a firm believer that mindfulness is a superpower. If you are not familiar with what mindfulness is, mindfulness is the practice of being in the moment without judgment. It is about being present with your thoughts rather than allowing them to travel to the past or future. I teach my clients about learning to be 10% in the past, 80% in the present and 10% in the future. As counselors, we call this 10-80-10, and we use this with our clients. One of my favorite TED Talks is "How Mindfulness Meditation can redefine Pain, Happiness and Satisfaction" (2014). In this TED Talk, Dr. Kasim Al-Mashat shares his experience of living with monks at a Buddhist Monastery. He tells how he had to live in silence for months while practicing meditation for 14 hours a day in the heat. Dr. Al-Mashat explains how practicing mindfulness meditation can help one to experience happiness and life satisfaction, not in the future or in things, but right here and now (TED, 2014). He shares how it all begins with our minds. Happiness is all in your head. If one is not mindful, then they will miss all that is transpiring around them. They will be anxious about the future or depressed about the past (or both). They will never be content with themselves or with what they possess. They will always be searching for happiness. But happiness is not outside of us, it is within us and our present state. That is why they say *the present is a present*; it's a gift.

Learning mindfulness has been one of the best ways to help me understand my feelings and behaviors. Once I am able to understand why I feel

45

the way I do, I can then practice my other techniques to alleviate my issues. For example, sometimes I get angry with my children for not obeying me. I think this is normal for most people. If I am not being mindful, I will quickly lash out and raise my voice at them. On the days where I am more mindful, I stop myself and ask why I am truly upset. Sometimes it is because I am tired or sad about something. Sometimes I'm hungry or have PMS. Sometimes I feel disrespected, or my thoughts are preoccupied with other matters. These are all particularly good reasons to be upset, but not good reasons to lash out at my kids. Yes, the child did not obey, but they don't deserve for me to yell at them because I'm not feeling well. I know this book is not about communication, but mindfulness can definitely help us to be better communicators. Mindfulness helps us to figure out what we're struggling with so we can take care of it.

I am sure you have heard of H.A.L.T.: Hungry, Angry, Lonely, and Tired. We use this acronym in addiction because it helps us to be more mindful of how we are feeling. When in a group setting, I have my clients write down how they are feeling that day. Taking a moment to figure out how you feel every day, has probably not been a priority for you. I am hoping you will take the time to stop and figure out how you feel, especially when you're feeling your cravings and urges. When you have a craving, it may be because of something that has happened that made you feel embarrassed, ashamed, or sad, which leads to the secondary emotion: anger. Let me state this sentence backwards. When you feel the secondary emotion of anger, you then become mindful and realized that you felt embarrassed, ashamed, or sad. You have a neural pathway already that says you don't like feeling that way, so you began to crave your drug. Recall the chapter on neuroscience of the brain. For so long you have been numbing those negative feelings with drugs that your brain has created those neural pathways to be automatic.

Neural Pathway: Negative feeling = Drug desire

Where's mindfulness in that equation? I bet there hasn't been any mindfulness in your life for a very long time when it comes to your cravings. If you want to read a good book, it's called *The Craving Mind,* by Dr. Judson Brewer. Dr. Brewer is a neuroscientist who studies how mindfulness can be used to reduce cravings. In fact, Dr. Brewer ". . . found that the modified version of MBRP [Mindfulness-Based Relapse Prevention] worked as well as cognitive behavioral therapy (CBT) at helping people not relapse into alcohol or cocaine use" (Brewer, 2017, p.25). After reading Dr. Brewer's book, I found that mindfulness played a huge factor in relapse prevention which is why I highly recommend mindfulness when learning to break free from our shame.

Shame plays a role in why we continue to use. If we can practice being more mindful of why we feel the way we feel, especially the feeling of shame, it can help us reduce our cravings. Like I said, mindfulness is a superpower. It helps us to take a step back and assess our situation, so we won't automatically go into fight, flight, or freeze, but rather it helps us to be more logical. I am not going to lie, I'm not always mindful. Just the other day I completely lost it when I found out my 15-year-old son was playing a video game that we already told him not to play. Let us just say I think I might have given my foot a hairline fracture. I'm not perfect. Obviously, you aren't perfect, and that's okay! One of four agreements in Dr. Ruiz's book is: "Always do your best" (Ruiz, 1997, p.75). Dr. Ruiz explains that if we always do our best (some days may not be as good as others, but that's okay), we won't have the opportunity to feel guilty, blame ourselves, or feel ashamed because we can say, "I did my best" (Ruiz, 1997, p.80). I felt bad that I overreacted in response to my son, especially since I am a counselor and know how to be mindful. I could have judged myself and told myself how I should be ashamed for what I did. It's something I used to do. I used to tell myself to be ashamed a lot. This time, I admitted my fault to my kid and gave myself a bit of grace for not having a good day. My intentions were good in that I love my son and want to see him succeed in life. I did my best that day.

Take time out today and practice being in the moment. If you have kids, hug them a little longer than usual. If you garden, enjoy the feel of the dirt between your fingers. If you are working on your car, take a moment to smell the gas and oil. Taking time out to enjoy the small things. Showing gratitude for those things will help you improve your mindfulness as well as help improve yourself. Also, when you start to feel a craving or an urge to use, take a moment to be mindful. How do you feel? Why do you feel that way? Ask yourself, "What is going on right now that is driving this craving?" Maybe it was a situation or H.A.L.T. (hungry, angry, lonely, tired). Either way, you are beginning to change your neural pathways!

Mindfulness Meditation

I want to mention mindfulness meditation as an honorable mention because it has helped several of my clients. I hope you will take the time to watch Dr. Al-Mashat's TED Talk (2014) as mentioned earlier. He describes mindfulness meditation in a way you will understand, and the benefits he describes are amazing.

If you are thinking, *Wait a minute! Meditation? I don't think so,* then hear me out. I have had several clients tell me they have never meditated before. They were skeptical, but because it was an addiction treatment facility, they were required to meditate. Many of my skeptical clients would come to me and tell me how great meditation was for them as they practiced it. I received comments such as: *I feel more calm. I was able to get to sleep quicker. I've never meditated before and didn't think it worked, but this is amazing!* I have had all these comments and more with my clients.

Mindfulness meditation is a wonderful practice which will help you to work on being more mindful and in the moment. Just like anything, it takes practice. I have had several clients with ADD/ADHD. They have mentioned how it is difficult for them to practice meditation. If you have ADD, there is hope. People with ADD generally have a slow alpha brain wave. Let me explain what an alpha brainwave is in our psychology world.

I am going on a small tangent, so bear with me. I used to be a Neurofeedback Technician. In Neurofeedback, we attach the client's brain to a computer. The computer reads the brainwaves and lets the client know if their brainwave is on the right frequency. If it is not, it will signal to the client either through sound or sight, depending on the program, that the client needs to relax for the program to get back on track and train the brainwaves to get on the right frequency.

Let me share with you Brainwaves 101. Brainwaves are electrical impulses in the brain. A person generally has five different brain waves: Delta, Theta, Alpha, Beta, Gamma. Each brainwave tells your body to be in a certain state and do certain things. Delta says, *it's time to have deep sleep.* This is when your spinal fluid comes up and washes over your brain and cleans out the proteins and other "stuff" that has been piling up throughout the day. Delta also signals to your body that it needs to heal itself. Theta is your REM (rapid eye moment) brainwave. This tells your body—*it's time to dream.* Dreaming helps the brain to download and process information. It takes events from your life and tries to make sense out of it. While I don't think dreams make sense, that is what your brain is doing. There is also the Alpha brainwave. This brainwave is the one that helps you feel relaxed, focused, and "in the zone." You'll notice that when you go to sleep, you'll start to dream but you're still somewhat awake. This is called Alpha-Theta sleep. It begins the process of delving into Delta sleep. The Delta and Theta brainwaves are essential to having a good night's sleep. Your brain will have 2-4 cycles during sleep where the brainwave moves from Delta to Theta, back to Delta, and then back to Theta. You probably recognize that in the night you'll dream around certain times but not other times. However, if you are like me, you might go from Delta to Theta, move up to Alpha, and then go back to Theta before eventually returning to Delta. This type of sleep can be annoying as you will constantly wake up throughout the night. Sleep is important, especially when you're trying to deal with your cravings and urges. I suggest seeing a doctor if all else fails with your sleep issues. Getting good sleep can help aid you in your sobriety.

In addition to the Alpha brainwave, I wanted to share with you an interesting aspect of it. This is the brainwave that for most people with ADHD is too slow, MHz (Megahertz). MHz is a unit of frequency. This brainwave is the best because it tells our brains to produce dopamine. We all love dopamine because it makes us feel good. We get it every time we think about our next addiction fix. Have you noticed that when you get a craving or an urge for your drug of choice, you will plan out when you can have that next "fix," and then you instantly feel a little better? This is what dopamine does for us—it helps us feel better for a time. The Alpha brainwave helps us become relaxed, feel good, and stay focused. If you recall from earlier, the parasympathetic system which is the "rest and digest" system, is associated with the Alpha brainwave. For those with ADHD, it's difficult to stay in the parasympathetic system, and it's difficult to stay focused. This is because their Alpha brainwave is too slow, and they're not getting the dopamine they need to relax. However, there are times when they can hyper-fixate on certain tasks and stay focused. That is a whole other story, but I wanted to mention ADHD because many people with this condition use drugs or alcohol to help tame their symptoms.

Let's not forget to mention Beta and Gamma brainwaves. Beta helps us to *stay awake and alert*. Beta is probably what you are in now as you read this book. Oh, I hope you are in Beta and not Theta! I hope this book isn't too boring! As for Gamma, this is where you are *hyper-focused*. This is when people are doing extreme sports or maybe you are extremely angry. This brainwave is usually in the sympathetic system. The sympathetic system is the fight, flight or freeze system. You are usually hyper-alert, hyper-aware, and extremely focused when in this brainwave. I guess you could call it *being in the zone* for some people.

Now that you know about the five different brainwaves, you hopefully have a better understanding of what they do for us. Sometimes brainwaves can get on the wrong frequency, hence ADD and the Alpha brainwave being too slow. When brainwaves are on the wrong frequency, it can cause problems such as ADD, sleep problems, memory problems, flashbacks, anxiety, depression, etc. Brainwave frequencies can be disrupted due to genetics, brain injuries, the substances we put in our bodies, or how we take care of our bodies in general.

Here is the good news, we can train our brainwaves to get back onto the right frequencies. Neurofeedback is one way we can do this. I am sure that if all of us go and get Neurofeedback and pay 100 dollars a session, then we will be good! Oh, and by the way, we need about 40-60 sessions in order for Neurofeedback to be the most effective. Now if you have the money or the insurance to pay for it, then I highly recommend Neurofeedback. However, what if you don't? Here is the better news! You don't need Neurofeedback to change your brainwaves! It's time-consuming, but it's worth it! *And what is it,* you ask? You ready for this . . . ?

Yes, I am bringing it back to: Mindfulness Meditation. That was quite the tangent, but I think it is particularly important for you to understand how brainwaves work and what they do for us. Studies have shown how mindfulness meditation can help people not only with ADD, but with various mental illnesses.

I try to meditate at least 10 minutes a day using YouTube meditations. I have even created my own meditation channel called Serene Meditation by Amanda Harms. A few of my clients enjoyed my voice when I facilitated meditations in group, and they wanted to listen to me when they went home. I created a few meditations for them to listen to. I encourage you to try out meditations daily, preferably the mindful ones as they will help you practice your mindful meditation.

CHAPTER 10

To Be Vulnerable or To Not Be Vulnerable: That Is the Question.

I asked my clients in group, *What makes you feel vulnerable that leads you to use?* Here are some of the things they shared:

> Boredom. Not feeling accepted by friends. The pressure of having to take care of family. My body image. Fear of failure. Anxiety. Depression. Finances. Family. My job.

I am sure you have experienced some of these types of vulnerabilities and perhaps have others as well. What does vulnerability mean to you? Dr. Brown shares from the Merriam-Webster dictionary that vulnerability can mean "capable of being wounded" or "open to attack or damage" (Brown, 2012, p.39). Many of us have been brought up to think, *Vulnerability is a weakness,* but Dr. Brown says otherwise, that vulnerability is a strength (Brown, 2012, p.33). Dr. Brown found that "vulnerability isn't good or bad: It's not what we call a dark emotion, nor is it a light, positive experience" (Brown, 2012, p.33). Rather, vulnerability is necessary if you want to become a wholehearted person. If you recall from a previous chapter, a wholehearted person is one who believes they are worthy of love and belonging as well as believes in ". . . hope, empathy, accountability, and authenticity" (Brown, 2012, p.34).

We are so afraid of failure, criticism, judgment, imperfection, etc. that we numb being vulnerable to those things. And how do we numb? Through our drug use. It becomes a vicious cycle. We start to feel vulnerable, and we can't handle it. Then we numb ourselves, and then feel shame about ourselves. We crawl into our hole and stay there until we feel the need for connection. Then we come out of our hole and begin to feel vulnerable, so we numb ourselves and again feel shameful about it. Here is the cycle:

Being vulnerable is not an easy task sometimes but being vulnerable is necessary to live a full life. "Vulnerability is the birthplace of love, belonging, joy, courage, empathy and creativity" (Brown, 2012, p.34). Many of us have been trying to avoid vulnerability at all costs because sometimes the feelings associated with vulnerability hurt. The problem is that when you numb all the hurtful feelings, you are also numbing all the positive feelings as well. Let me repeat that again differently: When you numb the bad, you are also numbing the good. You would be surprised at how many of my clients were shocked when they realized they were numbing everything when they used. If you were surprised by this, good, because you learned something new. If you already knew this, then you're ahead of the game. "To feel is to be vulnerable" (Brown, 2012, p.33). Feeling the "feels," both good and bad is how wholehearted people live a full life. Feeling the "feels" is extremely important when it comes to vulnerability. I am going to explain more about feeling the "feels" in a later chapter.

Being vulnerable is one of the most important ways to build shame resilience and break free from shame. Vulnerability is a strength in that most people who are vulnerable are living life without fear. I remember watching a famous Late-Night TV show host who filmed part of his shown in Cuba. As I watched him dance around with the locals, I thought to myself, *I can't believe this guy, who can't really dance, but would get up and dance in front of millions of people.* I continued to watch and could tell he was having a good time. Here this guy is acting "like a fool" and is having a good time. Okay, fair enough that he is getting paid a lot to do his show, but how many of us would get up and dance in front of millions of people? I can only relate on a much smaller scale. There was a school dance that my elementary school children had wanted to attend. It was a family dance, so I took them, but I didn't know anyone at the dance. I felt silly and out of place. I guess you can say I was feeling vulnerable. My 10-year-old daughter said, "Mom, come dance with us." I looked around the gym and noticed that all the parents were lined up against the wall either on their cell phones or talking to each other. The children were, of course, dancing their little hearts out on the gym floor. I had a decision to make. I could lean into my vulnerability or build a brick wall and make an excuse as to why I wasn't able to join my daughter out on the dance floor. I chose the former. I got out on the dance floor and started dancing with my kids. I may have taken dance when I was 9 years old, but I don't remember anything, and my dancing is pretty low grade. However, I danced for over an hour with my children. I was the only parent dancing, but toward the end, I saw a couple of other parents get out and dance. I actually had fun, and here's the best part: My daughter came up to me and said, "Mom, you're the best mom ever, because you came out and danced with us and the other parents didn't." Wow! I was glad I chose to be vulnerable.

Vulnerability = Connection

I connected with my daughter, and it was a beautiful thing. Do you see how vulnerability can be a strength? Vulnerability helps us grow and connect. "If we want greater clarity in our purpose or deeper and more meaningful spiritual lives, vulnerability is the path" (Brown, 2012, p.34). If we want to be wholehearted, we must be willing to be vulnerable.

I must mention something especially important when it comes to vulnerability. One part of building resilience to shame is to share our shame with others. This is vulnerability at its core. "Shame hates it when we reach out and tell our story. It hates words being wrapped around it–it can't survive being shared" (Brown, 2010, p.9). Dr. Brown says that if we do not talk about our shame, the more shame we will have. The antidote to shame is empathy because empathy is how we connect with others and how we can break free from shame (Brown, 2012).

One day, I called my friend and we chatted about our children and our lives. I told her about my financial struggles our family has dealt with for the past 20 years. This was difficult for me, as I have felt so much shame from this trial in my life. However, I knew I could share this with her because she has always been incredibly supportive and understanding. She empathizes with my struggles because she has been in the boat of financial hardship before. Empathy is more than just saying I'm sorry that happened to you, it's saying, That really sucks! I know how you feel, and I'm here for you. Actually, I did not realize how much shame I had about our financial situation until after I spoke with my friend, but I was able to feel and share my shame without feeling more shame. My friend did not shame me more, but rather helped me feel better about my circumstances.

Here's the catch: "We have to own our story and share it with someone who has earned the right to hear it, someone whom we can count on to respond with compassion" (Brown, 2010, p.9). I don't think you'd want to go around and tell just anybody about your shame. To hear your shame, it must be someone who has earned the right to hear it. It must be someone who can provide empathy and compassion.

When I run my addiction and recovery groups, I hear from my clients how nice it is to be in a group where people understand what they are going through. They feel safe sharing their shame and feel understood because the other clients have been through the same thing they are going through. If you are unsure who to be vulnerable with to share your shame, I encourage you to attend the Church's 12 Step meetings. It may feel shameful at first to attend, but soon you will find others who completely understand what you are going through. You will find a safe place to share your shame and feel understood.

I hope you were able to understand the power of vulnerability. This chapter is a small summary of what vulnerability entails, but know that vulnerability is part of the foundation we are trying to create to break free from our shame. I encourage you to take the time to reach out to someone you can trust and share some of your shame. If that is too difficult, then write your shame in a journal. I also encourage you to take more chances, feel your feelings, speak up in a group setting–anything that makes you feel vulnerable. It is a great practice if you want to live life to its fullest.

CHAPTER 11

DEFENSE MECHANISMS A.K.A MASKS

What is a defense mechanism, or a mask? Here is my definition of a defense mechanism: A defense mechanism is a covert behavior that is used to deflect any type of attack, whether it's external or internal, which ultimately covers up deep felt emotions. Some psychologists call these masks. Masks are used to cover up what is behind it. I am talking about masks that can't be seen but are very real because they cover up the truth. We all wear masks. I may be having a bad day, but at work I put on a smile and act like nothing is wrong. People then ask me, *How are you doing,* and I reply, *I'm good, thanks for asking,* but deep down I'm not feeling my best emotionally. This is a mask I wear. These masks are normal. We all use these masks because we do not want to feel vulnerable. We need to be careful with whom we are vulnerable with, so we put these masks on to protect ourselves.

Not all masks are bad, like the one I have described above. As I've said, we can't just be vulnerable with anyone. We do need to protect ourselves at times and wearing masks helps protect us. The catch is that there are certain masks we wear that *can* hurt us. These are the masks of pride, perfectionism, judgment, denial, and playing the victim. These are the main ones I want to talk about because they are the most damaging of all masks.

But what do defense mechanisms or masks have to do with addiction? I am pretty sure that if you have an addiction, you have used one of these masks. I am guessing that most people do not want other people to know about their addiction unless that someone is close to them. What is awful about these masks is, believe it or not, they help keep you in your addiction. For example, when you have your mask of perfectionism on, you tend to focus on making things "perfect" so that you can avoid anxiety or the negative feelings of unworthiness you feel from "not being perfect." These negative feelings make you feel shameful and vulnerable, and if you don't have the skills to work through your vulnerability, you will use your addiction to numb the shame. Vulnerability, there is that word again. It is true, masks can be really good at hiding shame. Secrecy is necessary in order for shame to thrive, says Dr. Brown (2010). Masks are a good way to hide and keep shame a secret. Let us dive a bit deeper into each mask mentioned above.

Pride. "Pride is the universal sin, the great vice" (Benson, 1989). We have been warned to ". . . beware of pride, lest ye become as the Nephites of old" (D&C 38:39). President Benson shared in his April 1989 talk that pride is enmity. When one has enmity, they are usually opposed or hostile to something or someone. Those who are opposed or hostile are generally concerned with their own interests and desires rather than what the Lord desires for them. Pride can be deceptive in that it blinds us to what is truly important in our lives.

Pride is an interesting word. I think there should be another word in the English language for pride since there are so many different definitions. There's pride as in a lion's pride. Then you have being proud of your family or country type pride. This is a feeling of being pleased and grateful or what is called authentic pride. Lastly, there is pride as in a feeling of boastfulness, arrogance, or haughtiness. This pride is most commonly known as hubristic pride. I am going to speak of hubristic pride.

When I think of pride, I am reminded of the story of the monkey's hand in the jar. If you recall, there was a monkey who wanted the treat in the jar. Instead of tipping the jar over to retrieve the treat, the monkey would put his hand in the jar, grab the treat and then pull his hand up. The problem was that when his hand was in fist form, it would not fit back through the hole in the jar. The monkey had a dilemma. He either had to let the treat go and have his hand back or hold on to the treat and keep his hand and the treat in the jar. Unfortunately, the monkey would do the latter and would not let go of the treat. Sometimes we are like the monkey with his hand clinched around the treat. We get so prideful that we won't let go. Pride hinders us by not letting us use both hands. Hubristic pride is like a prison. We are never truly free if we don't let go of it.

According to Dieter F. Uchtdorf of the Quorum of the Twelve Apostles, pride is the sin of comparison, self-elevation, a deadly cancer, contention, and can turn into envy (2010). Pride keeps us from progressing spiritually and especially keeps us from truly connecting with our Savior. In fact, pride destroys the spirit which then leads us to spiritual darkness. I'm sure many of us have been in spiritual darkness where we feel cut off from the Lord, or unsure where or what to do. Perhaps you're there right now, and it may be pride-related or not, but you do have a mask that is keeping you from progressing spiritually.

If one is mindful enough, they can detect their own pride that is hindering them from growing spiritually. Pride is an excellent mask that hides many kinds of shame, even the shame of addiction. Are you ready and willing to let go of your pride and get the help you need? It means being vulnerable and can be scary, but letting go of pride is so freeing and wonderful! Do you recall the story of Alma the younger who went around persecuting the church? An angel appeared and asked him why he was being wicked. Alma fell and was unconscious until he woke up in his father's house filled with joy because he could feel his pains no more. Alma shared his story with his son, "Yea, I say unto you, my son, that there could be nothing so exquisite and so bitter as were my pains . . . that on the other hand, there can be nothing so exquisite and sweet as was my joy" (Alma 36:21). Alma is sharing the freedom he felt from letting go of his sins and his pride.

Pride is a mask that keeps us from feeling our feelings and digging deep within us. We must dig deep within in order to humble ourselves and become one with the Savior. This is especially difficult for people with Narcissistic Personality Disorder (American Psychiatric Association (2017). I mention this disorder because pride is the biggest mask in narcissistic personalities. If you are reading this, and you have narcissistic tendencies as described in a previous chapter, I encourage you to keep reading and practice the techniques given in this book. Like I have said before, it's going to be a hard and difficult journey and sometimes scary, but the freedom from addiction and shame is amazingly exquisite! "And the remission of sins bringeth meekness, and lowliness of heart; . . . [then] cometh the visitation of the Holy Ghost, which Comforter filleth with hope and perfect love, which love endureth by diligence unto prayer" (Moroni 8:26). I encourage all to take this journey of self-healing and break free from your shame by letting go of the mask of pride!

Perfectionism. I am not talking about OCD. I had a client who had been sexually abused as a child. As a grown up, she has been battling alcohol and has been to treatment a few times. She shared how she would try to be perfect as a child so that no one would notice how she was feeling on the inside. As an adult, she would do the same thing–try to be perfect. If people saw how perfect she was, then she could hide her shame from them. The problem with this, is that no one can be perfect, except for the Savior of course.

Perfectionism is a ruse in being human. It is deceptive and only causes problems. I want to mention the difference of perfectionism as a mask and being perfect. I know the scriptures read, "Be ye therefore perfect, even as your Father which is in heaven is perfect" (Matthew 5:48). We are commanded to be perfect, but not entirely in this life. Becoming perfect is a progression, and we can only be perfected in and through Christ. This means the Savior is the only way we can become perfect because of His wonderful love and the power of His Atonement.

Perfectionism as a mask is different than becoming perfect through Christ. Perfectionism says, *Look at me, I have my hair done, makeup on, the kids are dressed perfectly, they aren't fighting, my house is clean, I just got off of work and made a five course meal, etc., etc., etc.* You are so busy trying to look good for everyone else that you don't take the time to "look good" for the Lord. You're not taking the time to feel your feelings and dig deep within yourself to allow the Lord to work within you and help you to become the person He wants you to become. Another problem with perfectionism is that you will always fall short and never be good enough. You will never be smart enough, pretty enough, rich enough, etc. This mask keeps you in your shame and in your addiction.

Letting go of perfectionism is just as difficult of letting go of pride. First, you must be mindful of your perfectionism and slowly let it go piece by piece. It will be hard to practice feeling your feelings at first. It will be hard to dig deep within yourself, but you deserve to break free from your shame and know that you are enough.

Judgment. Yes, this is a form of pride. I think it is worth mentioning though because we need to discuss who is the worst judge in your life. If you just thought "I am," then you are correct. We are our worst judges. How many times have you criticized yourself for something? I am sure it's been a lot. Judging yourself is a great mask you can use to cover up digging deep within yourself.

With judgment also comes comparison. We judge others all the time to make ourselves feel better. *Well Randy drinks on the weekends and he still goes to church with his family. I only take a few opioids to get by during the day. I'm better than he is because I don't drink.* We have all had these types of thoughts to compare ourselves with others in order to feel better about ourselves. The mask of judgment only hurts us from truly getting to know ourselves as well as connecting with the Savior.

Playing the victim. What does it mean to play the victim? According to the Merriam-Webster Dictionary, the word victim means, "one that is acted on and usually adversely affected by a force or agent." We are all victims in a way because not everything goes our way in this world. I have had patients who have been abused, and use that abuse to grow, learn, and become better people because of it. I have also had patients who continue to use their abuse as an excuse to stay in their addiction. The latter patients are those who continue to play the victim. When you are in victim mode, you cannot change. Your thoughts will usually be more absolute such as, *This always happens to me, or I never get a break.* Thinking in absolutes, all or nothing, keeps people stuck in their addiction.

If you are an all or nothing thinker, you may want to be more cognizant of the victim mask. Victims do not heal. You may be, or may have been, a victim, but playing the victim will not help you to break free from your shame and addiction. I believe the opposite of victimhood is empowerment. Those who are mindful of their victim role and choose to stop saying, "Poor me" have chosen to be empowered. They have chosen to focus on what they can control and to do their best.

The problem is that people who use this mask in their addiction are so caught up in playing the victim that it becomes second nature to them. It is so much easier to play the victim. People who play the victim tend to get more sympathy from others in order to help themselves feel better. They are able to give more excuses to others which justify their behaviors. They don't have to face what is truly going on inside of them. They can easily put the blame on others without having to suffer the consequences. They are deflecting their emotions, which keeps them in their addiction.

I encourage you to be more mindful of your victimhood behavior. It may be that you have lost friends due to your playing the victim. Many people get tired of hearing the same "poor me" attitude and eventually ignore you. People feel powerless when they are around you because they will constantly try to help you, but you never seem to be helped. Finally, people get fed up and set boundaries with you and with themselves. They want to help but realize they can't help the person if the person doesn't help themselves.

Take steps to empower yourself for change. You may be, or may have been, a victim, but to play the victim will only keep you in your addiction. When you start taking responsibility for your thoughts and actions, you will start to feel something amazing. It is a feeling of authentic pride and a strong sense of self-worth. Empowerment feels good and is one way to help with breaking free from shame.

Denial. Denial is a mask of rationalization. It falls in line with judgment and comparison because you are denying what is real and true. We tend to rationalize or deny there is a problem to avoid the consequences. I am sure you have used this mask a few times. I have heard clients say, *I only binge on the weekends,* or *I have to take my pills so I can get through the day.* They deny there is a problem, because as soon as they admit there is a problem, then they are not the victim anymore. Now, they have to change, but sometimes they don't want to change which is when they head right back into denial.

On a quick side note, change is scary. I think most people with an addiction may want to change but know how hard it can be to do so. Anything worthwhile is going to take a lot of hard work. The question is: Are you ready to work hard? Are you ready to change? I hope so.

CHAPTER 12

SEND IT LOVE

This is one of my favorite sayings at work. I made a shirt that said, "Send it Love" and wore it to work a couple of times a month. If you watched Dr. Kasim Al-Mashat's TED Talk (2014), there is a part in the talk where he talks about the snakes at the monastery. Dr. Al-Mashat asked about the snakes and the monk tells him to walk mindfully, use a flashlight at night, and the best part, "Send them love" (TED, 2014). Dr. Al-Mashat said he was not ready to hear that last bit. Send the snakes love, what does that mean?

As children, our simple minds, or our reptilian brains, tell us to either like something or to hate it, whatever it may be. If it serves us well, we will like it and store that in our brain as something good. If it does not serve us well, then we think it's "bad," we hate it, and store it in our brains as something bad. As we grow older, we develop abstract thinking and can understand things in different ways than we did as kids, but that reptilian brain never forgets. Think about touching a hot stove as a kid. You remember how it felt and now you avoid touching the hot stove as an adult. When something does not serve us well such as touching a hot stove, the pain sends signals to the reptilian brain which says, *Ouch! That really hurts! I hate this feeling!* Then we hate the fact that we got burned and hate the burning pain. We do this all the time when it comes to our negative feelings about things and circumstances.

How many times have you gone straight to your drug of choice after you have experienced a negative feeling? Think about it. I am sure it is more than you would like to admit. First of all, you have created neural pathways to automatically go straight to your drug, but it probably all began because you developed a hate for the negative feelings in the first place. This allows your reptilian brain to move right into fight, flight, or freeze mode. Turning to your drug of choice is fleeing away from your negative emotions.

We tend to hate anything that hurts us whether it is mental, emotional, or physical, because it doesn't serve us well. At least that is what we have agreed with ourselves as children. What do we do about it? I want to introduce a concept that may be foreign to you. This concept is not easy to implement at first. Like all things, it takes practice. Instead of hating the negative emotion, I want you to be present with it (mindful), lean into it, feel it, experience it. The next thing is to practice recognizing your thoughts. It is amazing how a thousand thoughts can come from one feeling. Recognize your thoughts, acknowledge they are there, and then come back to the feeling. Try not to allow your thoughts to take you down the rabbit hole. Many times, when we are in a negative state, the adversary will try to put thoughts into your head. It is important to recognize these thoughts as just thoughts and focus on the feeling. Lastly, I want you to send your negative feeling love and compassion. Imagine a little child getting hurt. You are sad that the child has gotten hurt, and you want to make the child feel better. So you give the child hugs and kisses. I am not asking you to hug and kiss yourself, I'm asking you to give your feeling compassion as you would a little child. Perhaps you tell yourself that everything will be okay or maybe you can actually feel the love in your heart. What you're doing is training your brain to create new neural pathways of loving the pain instead of hating it. You do not have to like the pain, just hold it with compassion instead. You are also kicking Satan out of your head as you give compassion instead of hate because Satan can't reside in a place where there is love! I guarantee you will feel better faster and help yourself build resilience to shame.

I want to give an example to illustrate my point. There was a time in my life where I was frustrated with our family's financial situation (yes, that has been one my trials for many years), and I couldn't take it anymore. I was crying hard and did not want the kids to see, so I went into my garage where it was dark and sat down. I began to allow my thoughts to head down the rabbit hole: *Why do I have to experience this again? I'm such a loser. I can't deal with being poor anymore!* Then this thought jumped into my head, *You should just go get a knife and slit your throat!* I was startled and taken back by what I just thought. I could not believe it! That wasn't my thought. I would never think of something so awful. I quickly jumped up and went into the house to get out of the darkness and prayed because I knew that thought was from the adversary. As I prayed, I began to let go of my pride and negativity and lean into the discomfort of my pain and send it compassion. I was then able to feel the comforting warm feeling of the Holy Ghost.

I know many of you have had similar experiences to having these thoughts from the adversary in your head. I know some of you have acted upon these thoughts. I know how painful it is to feel you are not worth love and belonging, especially from Heavenly Father. In fact, the shame of addiction is probably one of the worst feelings anyone can have in the Church. I know of a guy who told me his story about feeling unworthy of love and belonging. This young man shared how deep he was in his addiction with drugs and alcohol. He felt so inadequate and dejected that he decided to end his life. He owned a gun and made sure it was completely full of bullets. He put the gun to his head and pulled the trigger. It didn't fire. He tried it again, and it still did not fire. He said he tried it one last time and again, it didn't fire. He thought it was broken, so he shot the gun randomly from where he was sitting, and it fired. He decided to put the gun down and call someone. This young man told me he wasn't sure if there was a God, but if there was, He was definitely watching out for him that day.

I believe our loving Heavenly Father was watching out for him that day. I believe it was not his time to die, and that God had a purpose for his life. This young man has been clean for a while and has decided to join the military. He has an amazing personality that I know will help God's children. God knows this young man and loves him so much that He spared this young man's life. If only this young man was closer to the Savior and knew how much he is loved!

You may not believe this right now, but you are worthy of love and belonging, especially from your Heavenly Father. He loves you perfectly even though you are not perfect. All He asks of you is to keep trying to do your best. I know that part of you doing your best now is to be mindful and send yourself compassion, love, and grace. Too often we are our own worst judge or critic. It's time to be your own best friend who can empathize and show compassion for yourself. As you do this, God's Holy Spirit will testify to you of your own self-worth and belonging. It is a win-win; you are processing your emotions in a healthy way and you also get to feel God's love!

I want to talk about the word fear. I am adding this to the chapter because I truly believe that fear is the opposite of love. As a counselor, I take a lot of time trying to figure out why I feel the way I do. I guess it comes with the territory. If I get angry or frustrated about something, I will stop myself and ask: *Why am I so angry about this? Why is this bothering me?* Let me give an example: My older daughter and I are quite different personality-wise. Our personalities are almost opposite. I have this issue with wanting her to like me as a mother. I believe this is normal, however, I know I cannot make people like me. I began to ask myself *Why?* Why doesn't she like me? What is it about me she doesn't like? What is it that I want with this relationship? I then thought, *Do I want respect?* No. *Do I want acceptance?* Not necessarily. I kept asking myself why until I got to the bottom of what it was. Fear. I was afraid of disconnection from my daughter.

I think the root of all our insecurities, pridefulness, anger, anything negative, has to do with fear. Take a moment right now and think of something you are insecure or angry about. I want you to ask yourself *Why?* Keep asking yourself this until you hit the bottom of the issue. I would be willing to bet that the bottom of your insecurity or anger is fear. We are all afraid. We try to cover it up with our masks by acting like we are fine or angry or use pride to block it out, but deep down we are all scared. What are we afraid of exactly? I think the answer to that is disconnection from others. We are afraid of not being connected. If you look back to the chapter on shame, isn't that why we are here? We are here to learn how to build connection with others, because without others, we will not be able to make it back to our Heavenly Father. Our biggest connection needs to be with our Savior, Jesus Christ. Our spirits know what's up. Our spirits know that we need connection, but because of the veil that was placed over our eyes after we were born, we fear the unknown partly due to our weaknesses. The adversary wants us to fear the unknown. He wants us to fear everything because fear is the opposite of love and hope. The adversary cannot love because he is the opposite of God, and God is love.

The good news is that because of the restored Church of Jesus Christ and modern-day revelation, we don't have to live in the unknown. We know the plan of happiness. We know that Christ is central to the plan of happiness, and as we turn to Him and allow His grace and love to enter our souls, we will feel it. We will replace our fear with love. That is the key. Find out what makes us afraid and turn that fear into love and compassion. From there we can begin to grow our light within us and drive out the shame that binds us. Shame is fear. Fear is binding. Love is freeing.

This is so easy to say but so hard to do sometimes. I get that. I don't expect you to start loving every single thing in this world, but I do ask you to practice and keep trying. If you mess up, that's okay, you just keep trying. Sometimes people feel that they've failed at things, so they feel like they are a failure, and they give up. I tell my clients that failure is not failure if you have learned from it. Failure is a learning opportunity. Have you ever heard the quote by Thomas Edison? "I have not failed. I've just found 10,000 ways that won't work" (Ruth, 2015). Edison was referring to the light bulb. How grateful we are that he had 10,000 learning opportunities! The point I am trying to make is that life is not about perfection, it's about progression. Learning from our failures is progression. The best way to progress is to bring compassion with you in your progression. Compassion will keep you from going down the rabbit hole and help you learn from your learning opportunities.

Love heals. The more we love, the more we are healed. I am not saying if you have a disease and send it love, you will be healed, although it can help. I am saying love can help heal us inside. Love can erase the shame. God is love. He can work mighty miracles if you let Him. This means you need hope, faith, and charity. Charity is the pure love of Christ. Give yourself more compassion and charity. You deserve it. You are worth love and belonging.

Chapter 13

Positive Thinking

I read a book called, *Positivity* by Dr. Barbara L. Fredrickson (2009). Dr. Fredrickson and her colleagues conducted an extensive amount of research on positive thinking. The basic concept is to have a ratio of three positive thoughts to one negative thought; 3:1. Actually, she mentions a 6:1 ratio where you have six positive thoughts to one negative thought. However, she says a 3:1 ratio can work just as well.

Guess what positivity all begins with? Yep, mindfulness. Mindfulness is the first step to practicing positivity. You have got to be mindful of your thoughts if you are practicing positivity.

When I read this book, I thought I was already a fairly positive person. Wow, did my view change when I started to be more mindful. I did not realize how negative I was about myself, other people, and especially about bad drivers on the road. I began to practice Dr. Fredrickson's 3 to 1 ratio, where every time I had a negative thought such as, *Oh, I'm so stupid, why did I do that* or, *That jerk, he needs to pay attention to the road,* I would replace them with three positive thoughts. I began by telling myself, *I'm not stupid, sometimes things just happen,* or *That guy might be having a bad day.*

Sometimes it feels like you're lying to yourself because you've made an agreement with yourself long ago that you are stupid, so you have developed a deep core belief that you're stupid no matter what. Then when you try to tell yourself that you are smart, you feel like you are lying to yourself. Maybe you have an agreement with yourself that you are ugly, and for years you've been reinforcing your belief that you're ugly with your negative thoughts about yourself. Now if someone tells you you're beautiful or you try to tell yourself that, you won't believe it. Here is what I say to this: Start with baby steps.

Do you recall the 1991 movie comedy *What about Bob?* The movie stars Bill Murray and Richard Dreyfus. Richard Dreyfus character plays Dr. Leo Marvin, a psychiatrist, and Bill's character is Bob Wiley, who has several phobias. Dr. Marvin writes a book called *Baby Steps* and gives the book to Bob. Bob starts with baby steps, literally and eventually follows Dr. Marvin and his family on vacation. Bob ends up ruining Dr. Marvin's vacation, but eventually is cured from all his phobias. I laugh so hard at this movie every time I watch it, but the point of it is true. Sometimes we need to take baby steps to help us get to where we need to go.

What does this have to do with positive thinking? If you feel like you're lying to yourself and can't tell yourself that you are smart or beautiful or whatever it may be, then tell yourself this, *Maybe, I am smart. Maybe, I am beautiful. Maybe, I can do this. Maybe my boss isn't as mean as I think he is.* Start small with your positive thinking. Remember, you are not going to get this over night. None of these techniques are quick fixes. You have been having "quick fixes" for a while now, and it probably has only brought you misery. Anything worthwhile takes time, so cut yourself some slack and try to be patient. It took me a good six months to change my negative thoughts to positive thoughts without having to be mindful about it. Yes, it takes that long for your brain to create new and lasting neural pathways when it comes to positive thinking and addiction.

When you have time, practice being mindful about your thoughts, especially the negative ones and focus on replacing them with positive thoughts. It might be difficult at first, but you will begin to notice a change in yourself. You will notice you don't judge or criticize yourself or others as much. It is such a freeing concept. Imagine not having to be your own worst judge, but rather your own best cheerleader. Imagine not getting jealous at others or angry with others because now you are more at peace with yourself. This is how we combat shame. Shame entangles us with those negative dark thoughts. If we can replace them with positive ones, we can begin to replace the negative neural pathways with positive neural pathways. On top of that, we are fighting the powers of Satan that bind us in those negative thoughts. We are breaking free from those binds!

CHAPTER 14

LETTING GO

In Dialectical Behavioral Therapy, developed by Dr. Marsha Linehan in the early 1990's, she presents the concept called Radical Acceptance (Linehan, 2014). Radical acceptance is when you stop kicking against the pricks. Kicking against the pricks is a scriptural term. It stems from biblical times when a stick with a sharp point would prod the animal while plowing. The reason for the prodding was to forcefully encourage the animal to walk in the right direction so the lines in the crop fields would remain straight. Every now and then, the animal would kick against the prick and hurt itself. Basically, when the animal would rebel or fight against the prick, it would suffer for it. Jesus told Saul, "And the Lord said, I am Jesus whom thou persecuted: it is hard for thee to kick against the pricks" (Acts 9:5). For so long we have been kicking against the pricks, rebelling, or fighting against reality, and we have all been suffering because of it. Radical acceptance is when we choose to stop kicking and learn to let go of all that is keeping us trapped in the suffering. We learn to stop with our impulsive and maladaptive behaviors and accept what *is* rather than what *we want* things to be. It is learning to tell ourselves, *It just is what it is.*

Sometimes life can throw hard things at you. They say when it rains, it pours right? At age 23, I was busy with three small children at home and was trying to be a good homemaker. The monotony of taking care of a home and children ultimately fell into a routine where I became more concerned with myself than I was with my husband and family. My husband

69

and I started having communication problems and soon our marital bliss was more like marital blah. I recall being so angry with God. I wanted things to be my way and work out the way I wanted, and I wanted things to be happy and wonderful. I chose to kick against the pricks by yelling at God. Many times, I would get mad at Him and wonder why He did not answer my prayers—at least the way I wanted them answered. I felt alone and dejected. It wasn't until I learned how to let go and give it to God that I was able to allow the Lord's love for me to work in my life. I definitely learned patience, but, more importantly, I learned how to work with my Savior, instead of against Him.

I am sure there are times you feel as if God is not answering your prayers. I am sure you wonder why God allows bad things to happen, or why He just won't heal you from your addiction after you have asked Him so many times to help you. I am sure you feel forsaken by God. I know this feeling very well. I may not have been wanting to be cured from an addiction, but I have wanted to be cured from depression and other problems that He didn't take away from me. I can remember thinking, *Okay, this is really bad. There is no way God would allow this to get any worse.* And then it does get worse, and I would kick against the pricks. I would fight every possible fight there was to fight. I would get angry, depressed, and I would bargain; yes, all the stages of grief. Why would God allow such bad things to happen to me? Does He not love me?

Yes, God loves me, and He loves you very much. When I see my children go through hard times and struggles, I want to reach out and save them, but I know that they need to experience those struggles because it's the only way they will grow and learn. I have learned that Heavenly Father allows bad things to happen because of agency, and because He knows it is pertinent to our eternal progression. Bad things happen to good people. It is how we *react* to what has happened to us that makes the difference. We do not practice radical acceptance enough. For some reason it is hard for us to learn to let go of what we cannot control. That is the key right there; letting go of what we have no control over and act on what we do have control over.

Letting go is a difficult concept for most people. If you are the type of person who won't let go of anything, it may be the cingulate gyrus system in your brain is firing too much. This is a special part of your brain that if given too many electrical pulses, it will cause a lot of anxiety. The only way to alleviate the anxiety is to get your way. You have heard of people with

Obsessive-Compulsive Disorder (OCD) (American Psychiatric Association, 2017). They usually have too many electrical pulses firing within their cingulate gyrus system. Hopefully, this is not the case with you, and if so, you might want to read Dr. Amen's book *Change Your Brain, Change Your Life* (2015). In fact, if you end up trying a lot of these tools that have been given, but you are not feeling any changes, then I recommend you read Dr. Amen's book and get professional help from a psychiatrist. The brain can use any help it can get.

Learning to let go is a practice, and it all begins with, mindfulness. You knew that was going to come up, didn't you? Mindfulness is the key to learning to let go. One of my all-time favorite self-help books is *Letting Go: The Pathway of Surrender* (2018). Dr. Hawkins shares the basic concept on how to let go, or how to surrender your emotions. "To be surrendered means to have no strong emotion about a thing: It's okay if it happens, and it's okay if it doesn't" (Hawkins, 2018 p.21). For example, you get in an argument about your drug use with a loved one because they cannot seem to understand why you continue to still use. You start to get upset and frustrated because you believe they will never understand. Let us stop there. Their inability to understand your drug use is out of your control. You hope that one day they will be able to understand, but for now they don't, and it can be frustrating. Being mindful of why you are frustrated and angry can help you understand what you need to let go of. You need to let go of wanting your loved one to understand you. This is radical acceptance. You are accepting the fact you have no control over someone else, and letting go means you can be okay with them never being able to understand. It is difficult to do, but over time it is possible.

I really wish someone would have told me when I was younger that I did not have to be angry if I didn't want to. I was a particularly angry person. I think I developed it from my dad because he would get angry, a lot. I got married when I was 18 years old and thought I knew how to be in a relationship. I thought I could change my husband because we were in love, and I was right about everything. Boy, was I wrong. Our marriage could have been so much better if I had not gone into it with certain understandings and expectations. I would get mad at my husband for some of the littlest things such as the way he tied his shoes or was late to everything. He still is late to everything, but the point is, I would get angry because of my expectations not being met. I now expect my husband to be late, so I get dressed and work on other things until he is ready to go. I do not like being late, but I realize it's something I have to let go because I can't change him or control what he does. I can only control the way I react to it, and I choose to be happy, not frustrated, or angry. Trust me, I've been upset way too many times and it did nothing to change him.

Expectations are not all bad. We expect the sun to rise every morning, we expect to have food in our tummies in the morning, and we expect to be respected by others. Expectations can be a good thing as they help us to stay motivated in accomplishing our goals. Here is the difference: Expectations are good when you have control over the situation. When you don't have control over the situation or the person, expectations aren't great. For example, you expect to get sober. This is a great expectation because it is something you have control over accomplishing. You expect for your loved ones and friends to understand your addiction and be more understanding of your situation. Obviously, this is not a good expectation because you have no control over what other people think and do. When we learn to let go of our expectations that "aren't great," we will find freedom in radically accepting the situations we have no control over.

When it comes to letting go, we need to be mindful of pride. If you recall in the previous chapter on masks and defense mechanisms, you know that pride is a serious defense mechanism that shouldn't be taken lightly. In order to let go, you must relinquish your pride. Remember, letting go is not about who is right or wrong, it is about accepting things for what they are and feeling okay with letting go. It is okay if it does happen, and it is okay if it doesn't. Most importantly, letting go is giving your grievances and frustrations to God. *Lord, I can't handle this right now, so I'm letting it go and giving it to Thee.* We cannot do that if we hold on to our pride.

Another emotion is fear. I know I have talked about fear in the *Send it Love* chapter, but I think this topic is important to mention again. Fear is inside all of us. We are all afraid of something. Sometimes our fear stems from our core beliefs or agreements we made with ourselves when we were younger. It is time to let go of those fears. How can we just let go when the emotion of fear is just so strong? Perhaps you think, *Fear is an emotion that keeps me safe.* Well, yes and no. It may keep you safe from things, but it is preventing you from truly living life. It is preventing you from being vulnerable. There are three ways, that I am thinking of right now, that help us to let go fear. But before I tell you what they are, you need to first recognize what you are afraid of. Once you pinpoint your fear, you then work on sending it compassion (you recall this from the *Send it Love* chapter). Next,

72

we need to practice letting go of the fear and surrendering it to God. Lastly, you pray and ask the Lord to help you let go of your fear. It takes time but letting go of your fear will help you to feel free to live life to its fullest. One thing I've been afraid of my whole life is singing a solo in public. I have sung several solos in public, but each time I have been completely afraid. I decided to let go of my fear. Where am I now with my public singing? I am still in the practice stage of letting go, but I'm much better than I was, and I still enjoy singing.

I've written a lot about letting go and maybe you're thinking, *That sounds great and all, but these feelings are too much for me to just let go.* First, you are not your feelings. Your feelings are a part of you, but not you. Feelings are there to protect you and to bless you. They are amazing. Second, you are the master of your soul and are capable of being the master of your feelings. Sometimes though, we all need to experience intense feelings, especially when the feelings are the stages of grief. It is perfectly normal for a person to experience the stages of grief before they can learn to let go of their feelings.

If you are not familiar with Kubler-Ross's (2009) stages of grief, let me quickly explain. Elisabeth Kubler-Ross is a psychiatrist who discovered the stages of grief to help people understand what they go through in the grieving process. The stages are denial, anger, bargaining, depression, and acceptance. As humans, we all go through these stages when we are grieving. The stages do not necessarily go in that order, nor are they all the same length in time. Each stage can be from 30 minutes to 30 years. Sometimes people do not go through all the stages. They may go from anger to depression back to bargaining and then acceptance. Another thing to remember is that when one is using alcohol or drugs during their grief, they do not process stages as they would without drugs or alcohol. I had a client who came in for addiction of alcohol and she was going through the stages of grief while in treatment. Her husband had died two years previously, and because she was always under the influence, she could not process her grief in an adaptive way. She was now processing her grief in treatment.

The stages of grief are important to work through when sober. Grief may be over any loss you may have had, whether it is a loss of a job, pet, or a loved one. It is important that you work through the stages of grief, or you may be stuck in a stage for 30 years—I know I have seen it in some of my clients. The technique of letting go is a wonderful tool that will help you progress through your stages in a gentler manner. Feelings are difficult to deal with, but when we lean into the discomfort, feel the "feels," and give them compassion, we can process them gently and perhaps quickly instead of repressing them with our drug use.

Recognizing which stage of grief we are feeling gives us the opportunity to practice surrendering that grief to God. Remember, letting go is about releasing our imagined control over things we can't control and allowing God to control it for us. That is the first step. The second step is to learn how to be "okay" with that release of control. It's telling ourselves, *It's okay if it happens or not because it's all in God's hands.*

Here's the quick run-down of how we let go. We are first mindful of the thought, emotion, or situation. We notice it's there, and then we look at it without judgment and give it compassion. We say to ourselves, It's okay if it's there or not, or It's okay if it happens or not. Next, we hand it over to the Lord. Lastly, we divert our attention to something else—something more positive. Will the thought, emotion, or situation come back? You can count on it! You keep practicing this technique and over time it will get easier to "let go."

Letting go takes practice, just like mindfulness, vulnerability, sending love, and positive thinking. You can use the accompanying workbook found on my website to practice these skills. I hope you will take the time to be mindful of what you do not have control over and practice letting it go by giving the situation to God. It does not mean we can't dream or hope that things will happen the way we want them to. God wants us to hope for things that are for our good and for the good of others. We just need to learn how to be okay with His timing of things and not our own timing of when we want things to happen.

CHAPTER 15

BOUNDARY SETTING

There are so many people who do not practice good boundaries. There are all sorts of boundaries, but the boundaries I am talking about are emotional and spiritual boundaries. I worked with a counselor once who had terrible boundaries. She would constantly take calls from her husband at work (who also had co-dependency boundary issues) and talk to him instead of doing her work. She would call him from work too. The terrible thing about their relationship is that she was having an affair, and he knew about it. He would still call her at least three or four times a day. This co-worker would be in a session with a client and would start looking things up on her phone while the client was talking to her (I only know that because the client told me). I was new to the counseling profession and was shocked that my co-worker had such terrible boundaries!

Boundaries are put in place to keep us safe. It is the same as commandments. God gives us commandments to help keep us safe. Without boundaries and commandments, our lives would be a total mess. This may date me a little bit, but there was a seminary video back in 1993 called *Act for Themselves*. You can look it up on YouTube. There is a part in the video where the actor was excited to drive down the street in a Ferrari 308 GTB. There were no rules or laws, and he could drive as fast as he wanted. He drove down the road super-fast and saw a semi-truck coming in the opposite direction. The semi-truck swerved into the Ferrari guy's lane. Just as it looked like they were going to crash, the Ferrari guy was instantly back in his bedroom. The Ferrari guy learned a valuable lesson. Without laws, rules, or boundaries, one cannot truly be safe. The semi-truck guy did not do anything wrong because there was no law stating he couldn't go into that lane.

Without laws, rules, or boundaries, no one can be held accountable for their actions. It's like the scripture, "For it must needs be, that there is an opposition in all things . . . Righteousness could not be brought to pass, neither wickedness, neither holiness nor misery, neither good nor bad" (2 Nephi 2:11). Basically, Lehi is saying that there is no purpose in creation if there are no opposites. There is good and bad, and because of that, God has created laws for us to follow to keep us safe from the bad.

Sometimes we feel like these laws are keeping us from so much more. The Word of Wisdom is found in the 89th section of the Doctrine and Covenants. This section tells us to not drink wine or strong drink, coffee, and not use tobacco. It also shares in the section what we can eat that would be good for us. At times, especially when we are teenagers, we feel restricted by these "rules." We feel we are not free to make our own choices. This thinking however is deceptive. God gave us the Word of Wisdom to keep us free from all the negative consequences of these substances. We know what alcohol does to the brain and the liver. We know coffee contains tonic acid which is not good for the body. We know tobacco causes cancer and other ailments. When God gives us commandments, He is showing His love for us because He wants us to be healthy and happy.

God also gives us boundaries that we must set with each other emotionally. First, He gives the commandment to remain sexually pure until marriage. He then gives us the commandment to stay sexually pure in marriage. These commandments are beautiful in that they help our emotional well-being. Think about it, fornication and adultery have destroyed many lives emotionally. God also gave us the commandment to "love one another" (John 13:34). This commandment coincides with "judge not" (Matthew 7:1). How is it that we are to love one another when we are judging others? This commandment of love is amazing. If we all had more love in our hearts, imagine what this world would be like. Imagine if we didn't judge each other either. There is more to judging, but that is for another book. My purpose is to show you that commandments and boundaries are put in place to keep us safe and to enjoy life to its fullest.

Setting boundaries with yourself helps you to stay accountable for your actions. It helps you tell people how you want to be treated and receive the respect you deserve. It helps you to gain a stronger sense of self and break free from the shame that holds you hostage. If you have an addiction, I am guessing you probably are not the best with setting boundaries and sticking to them. There are different types of boundaries, and only you can decide which ones will work for you. Obviously, the boundaries include physical boundaries, spiritual boundaries, and emotional boundaries.

Physical Boundaries. Physical boundaries include what you put into your body, physical closeness with others, and how you take care of your body on the outside. For example, my boundaries include eating healthy and minimizing sugar and soda. I choose to keep the Word of Wisdom. I include exercise as a daily routine, and I dress casually and modestly. My love language is physical touch, so I make sure I hug someone in my family every day, if not all. I try to be cognizant of others' physical boundaries because I know not everyone loves hugs. I do not mind being touched, just not inappropriately. These are my physical boundaries. Actually, I was slapped on the butt one time in Junior High by another kid. I turned around and told him off. Why? Because my body is mine, and he has no right to touch it. I, of course, had made a physical boundary with myself previously and made sure I stuck to my boundary. I made the boundary with my own family members that we are not to physically hurt each other, and if that boundary is broken, then there are consequences.

Spiritual Boundaries. Spiritual boundaries include how to grow spiritually stronger in your life. It has been shown that spiritual ties help people to feel better. We must all be growing spiritually every day, otherwise we are digressing spiritually. My spiritual boundaries include reading scriptures daily, study the Come Follow Me curriculum, and constant prayer throughout the day. I also include service daily, by making family meals and trying to keep the house clean. Healthy spiritual boundaries should also include patience. Learning patience is a wonderful quality that I am still striving for, but I think I am understanding it a bit more.

Sometimes people want to attack your spirituality. This isn't good, but it's important to keep your spiritual shield strong and not attack back. Patience and understanding of others are the keys to maintaining your spiritual stamina. Standing for what you believe in, is an awesome boundary and one not to be taken lightly. Overall, spiritual well-being is extremely important. If you have been lacking in this area, that's okay. You can always pick it up today and get back on your spiritual journey of growing closer to the Savior and becoming like Him.

Emotional Boundaries. Emotional boundaries include how you behave, how you want to be treated by others, and how you use skills and tools that help you emotionally. Emotionally well-adjusted people know how to communicate and use their skills and tools to help them stay emotionally balanced. For example, I use my tools of self-love and letting go frequently. I give anything that is bothering me compassion, and I work on letting it go and surrendering it to God. If it is something I do have control over, I will work on finding solutions, whether it is asking my husband for help, the internet, or prayer. I use the tool of mindfulness to assess how I am feeling and why I'm feeling that way, so I don't lash out at my husband and children. When I have difficult days, I use positive-thinking and send myself extra compassion. Although, there are days I don't have it in me. I then allow myself to feel the "feels," and I take part of the day off. I also connect with a friend or family member weekly. If someone is abusive to me, I let them know that it is not acceptable, and their behaviors are abusive. I show people how I want to be treated by treating them with respect. This is how I take care of myself emotionally.

These are just three types of boundaries that we need to really be aware of when it comes to breaking free from our shame. The most important aspect of boundary setting is that you train people how you want to be treated. Assertive communication is the way you go about it; it is showing respect to others.

This may seem like a lot. It really is a lot of tools I have given you, but the good news is that you do not have to do all of them every day. Consider using the workbook I've provided on my website. Pick one for the day, week or month, and work on that skill. You are not in a race to perfectionism in this life. This life is about progression, not perfectionism.

CHAPTER 16

FORGIVENESS

Forgiveness is not for other people; it is a special gift just for you. When you forgive, you feel more at peace and more joy in your life. I believe the main person that we need to learn to forgive is ourselves. If you recall the mask of judgment, you know that you are your own worst critic. It is hard for you to forgive yourself. In fact, sometimes it is harder for you to forgive yourself than to forgive others. Dr. Ruiz writes, "Forgiveness is the only way to heal. We can choose to forgive because we feel compassion for ourselves" (1997, p.114). I like the part where he says we *choose* to forgive. He then writes about how being the Judge of ourselves is how we go against ourselves. We tend to beat ourselves up and abuse ourselves over and over. Dr. Ruiz says we need to stop and tell ourselves "That's enough! . . . I will no longer be the Victim" (1997, p.115).

Recall the mask of playing the victim in the previous chapter. When we do not forgive ourselves for what we have done, we tend to hash and rehash the past mistakes we have made. Remember what Dr. Ruiz said about animals—they don't do that. They make the mistake once, learn from it and move on. When we make mistakes, we continue to beat ourselves up over and over again. Think of the story in the *Bible* of Lot's wife. She looked back and then turned into a pillar of salt (Genesis 19:26). We must not look back. I believe Satan plays a good role in this rehashing of our past mistakes. When we are feeling down or negative, the adversary tries to remind us that we are "bad" and "not good enough" by having us relive our past.

This is a reason why mindfulness is so important. I have done things in my past that I am not proud of, and many times I would think about my past and beat myself up over it. When I discovered mindfulness, I recognized that I was thinking of the past. I would then tell myself that I have repented and think of something good instead. I am basically saying, *Satan, get out of my head. I've repented, and I'm done with you. Jesus has already forgiven me, and I've forgiven myself.* Do you see how mindfulness, positive thinking, self-love, vulnerability, letting go and setting boundaries played a role in that one statement? It is empowering! Guess what I am also doing when I think that statement in my head? I am creating new neural pathways in my brain which gives Satan less power over me.

Shame keeps us from forgiving ourselves. Shame says we won't ever be good enough so we must punish ourselves because that's what we deserve. Shame will not let us forgive because forgiveness is of God. It is a godly quality, and we need to learn to possess more of it. The Savior is the greatest forgiver of all time. He graciously forgives us of all our sins when we choose to repent and turn to Him. "Nowhere are the generosity and the kindness and mercy of God more manifest than in repentance" (Packer, 2010). The best part is that He will continue to forgive us of the same mistakes we continue to make if we choose to keep repenting. "Yea, and as often as my people repent will I forgive them their trespasses against me" (Mosiah 26:30). The Savior wants to forgive us, and His love and forgiveness are so unconditional, there is nothing He cannot overcome. "However many mistakes you feel you have made . . . you have not traveled beyond the reach of divine love. It is not possible for you to sink lower than the infinite light of Christ's Atonement shines" (Holland, 2012).

How do we forgive ourselves? It has to be one of the hardest things for us to do. Dr. Ruiz says, "First, we need to forgive our parents, our brothers, our sisters, our friends, and God. Once you forgive God, you can finally forgive yourself" (1997, p.115). Jesus says we must forgive everyone "seventy times seven" and that includes yourself (Matthew 18:22). I know I say we need to forgive, but the hurt we feel inside is so strong! Sometimes our pride is hurt. Sometimes we have been hurt emotionally. Sometimes our trust has been broken. Whatever may have happened, there is hurt, anger, and sadness. These feelings are strong. Again, the reptilian brain is saying, *I have to remember this, so I won't forget it! Because if it happens again, I need to be prepared!* Your emotions are not you. Your emotions are a part of you, they are there to keep you safe, and they are there to help you enjoy life.

The good news is that our mind and our spirit are stronger than our emotions and our brain. Our minds and spirits can overcome the natural man. Recall the scripture: "For the natural man is an enemy to God and has been from the fall of Adam . . ." (Mosiah 3:19). What is the natural man? When I am in group, I tell my clients that there's the mind (I think of it as the spirit) and then there's the brain (the body). I think of the brain, or body, as the natural man. The adversary and his followers did not receive bodies due to their rebellion up in heaven. They are jealous of the fact that you have a body, and they basically want to take it over. When we allow the brain, body, to be in control of our mind, that is when the adversary takes over. Have you ever had a black out from your drug use, and then you wake up the next day to discover that you did some pretty bad things? It is mostly likely that the adversary took control instead, of your spirit being in control.

We are here on earth to learn how to have telestial bodies. Living in these bodies is preparing us for terrestrial bodies and then ultimately celestial bodies. Our spirits must learn how to overcome the natural man, because "the natural man receiveth not the things of the Spirit of God" (1 Cor. 2:14). In order for us to be spiritually-minded instead of carnally-minded, because "carnally-minded is death," we need to work on being mindful of our thoughts and emotions (Romans 8:6). Of course, there is more to it than that, but I hope you can see how the mind can overcome the brain through all the tools and techniques I have given in the previous chapters.

What does this all have to do with forgiveness? I know I went off on a tangent, but forgiveness is learning to recognize or be mindful of the hurtful and resentful feelings you have toward others and toward yourself. Once those feelings have been recognized, you then practice sending them compassion. It is okay to feel hurt and pain. Instead of hating them and the person who hurt you, turn inward and send those feelings love/compassion. Tell yourself it is okay to feel that way. Sometimes we feel a certain way and think to ourselves, *I shouldn't be feeling this way!* The truth of the matter is that you are feeling that way, and it is there for a reason. We must replace the hate, hurt, fear, and all else that is not of God, with love and compassion. Every time those negative feelings come up about you or someone else, you continue to replace them with the positive feelings and thoughts. Along with prayer and the great love of the Savior, I guarantee that over time, you will start to notice love growing within your heart. It won't necessarily happen magically over night, but it will happen.

Sometimes people will do things that last for years, and this can include yourself and your addiction. Sometimes people do not change. It is hard to forgive people who show no signs of changing soon. I had a fellow student who was sexually abused by her stepfather. When she was older, she joined the military and moved away. She later confronted him about what he had done, and he denied everything. This was difficult for her because she knew what he had done, and God knew what he had done. She realized she needed to forgive him so that she could move on with her life. She said it was extremely difficult, but the freedom she felt from her anger was amazing and worth it.

There was a person in my life who would not change at all. I went through all the stages of grief and all the emotions, but to no avail, I could not change them. Ultimately, I had to forgive, let go and change myself. It is funny to think about me being the one who had to change, but it was incredible. I have learned how to forgive better and easier as well as be more understanding and thoughtful. It was when I *decided* to change and not "kick against the pricks" anymore, that I felt free from my hurt and anger. I chose to take complete responsibility for my actions and focus on what I needed to do rather than the other person. I guess forgiveness came when I learned how to empower myself instead of playing the victim. I'm not saying this will work for you, but I'm suggesting that you worry about yourself, empower yourself, take responsibility for your thoughts and behaviors. Let go of the other people's behavior. Yes, this is including your addicted self!

Easy to say and hard to do right? It takes time and lots of practice. Again, don't feel you have to do it all at once. Slow and steady wins the race when it comes to changing ourselves. With the help of the Savior, we can learn to forgive in deeper ways—ways that will heal our souls. You just need to be willing to give it a try.

Chapter 17

Godly Sorrow vs Worldly Sorrow

There is a story in the Book of Mormon where Mormon is the leader of the Nephite army. Mormon became the leader of the army at the noticeably young age of fifteen years old. Mormon was a righteous man who was saddened by the wickedness of the Nephites. In fact, there was a point that Mormon quit being the leader because of the Nephites wickedness. Mormon later returned to being their leader but wrote about the horrible scene that laid before his eyes. Mormon was commanded at first to preach to the Nephites, but when they did not listen and remained in their wickedness, the Lord told Mormon not to preach anymore. Then at one point during his command, the Nephites looked as if they were repenting. Mormon wrote:

> And it came to pass that when I, Mormon, saw their lamentation and their mourning and their sorrow before the Lord, my heart did begin to rejoice within me, knowing the mercies of the long-suffering of the Lord . . . But behold this my joy was vain, for their sorrowing was not unto repentance, because of the goodness of God; but it was rather the sorrowing of the damned, because the Lord would not always suffer them to take happiness in sin (Mormon 2:12-13).

The Nephites had become 'past feeling' insomuch that they would not turn to the Lord for their sorrow. They were sorry that they were suffering and in pain. They were sorry that they could not beat the Lamanites. They were sorry that so many of their brothers had died. Yet, they were not sorry they had disobeyed the Lord and not kept His commandments. This is worldly sorrow. This type of sorrow leads to death—spiritual death.

The Apostle Paul taught, "For godly sorrow worketh repentance to salvation not to be repented of: but the sorrow of the world worketh death" (2 Corinthians 7:10). Worldly sorrow is the opposite of Godly sorrow. "Worldly sorrow pulls us down, extinguishes hope, and persuades us to give in to further temptation" (Uchtdorf, 2013). Worldly sorrow is a big part of shame.

Shame says you are not worthy of connection, love, or belonging. Shame keeps us from having hope and drags us into despair. Worldly sorrow says you are not worthy of love and also keeps you from having hope. Worldly sorrow keeps you in despair.

Some of my favorite stories from the *Bible* are Saul and David, found in 1st and 2nd Samuel. King Saul was righteous and good at first. He was chosen to be King because of his righteousness. Of course, over time, Saul did not continue to follow the Lord, and he became wicked. There were points in Saul's life where he became sorrowful because David was better than him. He tried several times to kill David and was unsuccessful. He finally was killed along with three of his sons. King Saul had worldly sorrow. He was sorrowful about things that happened in his life, but he was never truly repentant. Because he did not turn to the Lord in a repentant manner, I think he fell into a type of despair. Saul was so desperate to speak to the Lord, or rather the prophet Samuel, that he went to the witch of Endor. After his encounter with the spirit Samuel, Saul was afraid. He was told that he would die the next day and that Israel will fall into the hands of the Philistines. Did Saul humble himself and turn to the Lord after that and repent? No. Worldly sorrow does not make you want to repent, nor does it draw you closer to the Lord. This is exactly how shame works as well. Shame does not want you to repent, nor does it draw you closer to the Savior.

When I studied King David, I fell in love with his story. I loved David's righteousness and goodness. He always tried to serve the Lord and do what the Lord would have him do. He was then blessed with great intellect and was highly favored of the Lord. Unfortunately, King David gave into temptation (just like we all do), and he tried to cover up his mistake by having someone killed. I am sure King David used a lot of rationalization to cover up his first mistake—committing adultery. He probably rationalized that if he put the woman's husband on the front lines of battle, that the husband will be killed, and it wasn't really David's fault. We tend to rationalize our drug use a lot to make it seem like it isn't that bad. However, the Lord knows better. He chastened David and took away some of his promised blessings. David felt sorrow, after he was chastened by the Lord through the prophet Nathan. David felt Godly sorrow. He lamented and felt bad about what he had done. He repented and tried to draw close to the Lord again, but David was never truly the same great king that he was before his mistakes. However, David's story gives us hope; hope that we can repent if we have Godly sorrow.

Guilt is an important part of this. Guilt says, *I'm sorry I did something bad.* It motivates us to want to change and be better. David felt tremendous guilt for what he had done, maybe some shame too at some point, but definitely guilt. He was able to have Godly sorrow for his sins and repent of them. Saul never did repent of his sins. "Godly sorrow leads to conversion and a change of heart. It causes us to hate sin and love goodness. It encourages us to stand up and walk in the light of Christ's love" (Uchtdorf, 2013). Guilt may not be a good feeling, but it is a good thing.

Think of Godly sorrow and guilt as leading you to repentance because Godly sorrow works repentance to salvation. Sometimes some of us look at repentance as a bad thing, because usually repentance happens due to someone doing something "bad." I really wish I could change everyone's thinking about repentance and help them see how it's a good thing. We all make mistakes because we are human, and mistakes or sins lead us away from the Savior. Repentance is what leads us back to the Savior. If the Savior is truth and light, and we want to draw close to the Savior, then how can repentance be bad? Repentance is beautiful and amazing. I believe some of us think the word repentance is bad because we associate it with shame. We feel shameful about our sin, and we know we need to repent, but the shame is so strong we do not feel we deserve to connect with the Savior. We wallow in our shame until it eats us up inside, and then we are forced to repent in order to feel better. The truth is, until we can break free from our shame, we will never truly feel better. Yes, we are supposed to feel bad for sinning, but only because it leads us to repent and feel forgiveness from the Lord. When we feel shame, we may feel forgiveness from the Lord, but it makes it harder to forgive ourselves. We then punish ourselves by committing the sin again and feeling shame for it. It becomes the cycle of shame.

I encourage you to look at repentance as a wonderful tool you can use to draw closer to your Savior and Heavenly Father. As you repent, with real intent, you will find that the burden of shame will become lighter and easier to bare, and hopefully it will dissipate altogether.

The reason I bring up worldly and Godly sorrow is because one tears us down into despair and hopelessness, and the other changes our heart and lifts us up toward our Savior. It can be the same with guilt and shame. Guilt motivates us to rise up, while shame takes away our hope and pushes us down. I want to encourage you to be mindful when you feel shame. Take a moment, tell yourself you are worth more than shame. Reach out and share your story with someone who has earned it, especially with Heavenly Father. Tell Him your struggles, thoughts, feelings, and everything else. He knows you. He knows you don't want to be stuck in your addiction. He has never been disappointed with you about it. Not once! God does not get disappointed. If he were disappointed in us, then that would mean we are not good enough, and that is not true! He cannot be disappointed in us because He already knows who we are and what we are going to do in our life. Sure, He can be displeased, but never disappointed. God knows your potential and knows you more than you will ever know yourself in this life. His hand is always stretched out toward you, waiting for you to take it and feel His love for you. He is always there. It is our job to feel Godly sorrow for our mistakes and turn towards Him. It is His job to love and forgive us and help us to forgive ourselves and others.

Does it mean we need to let go of our masks, especially the mask of pride? Yep! You will find that as you let go of your masks and give them to the Lord, He will strengthen you. "I give unto men weakness that they may be humble; . . . for if they humble themselves before me, and have faith in me, then will I make weak things become strong unto them" (Ether 12:27).

Humbleness, I believe, is one of the greatest virtues. Without it, we can never grow close to the Lord. In my definition, humbleness means you don't know it all. It means you are teachable. It means you are willing to let go of your masks. It means you are willing to change and grow according to what the Lord wants for you. It seems kind of scary to think about because if we become humble, it can feel as though we are letting go of our control. We are human beings and being in control of things is what we do. It makes us feel sane and powerful. When we lose control of ourselves and our lives, we feel lost and sometimes, crazy (for lack of a better word).

I want you to know that letting go of your masks and humbling yourself is the greatest power of control you will ever have over yourself and your life. You are making an agreement with yourself that you will allow the Lord to have dominion over your life. In essence, you are in control as you choose to allow the Lord to be in control of your life. Let Him take the helm of your life as you do what He asks of you. You will find that as you let go and humble yourself, as you give control of your life to the Lord, you will have more control over your life. It's an interesting concept, one of which you may have to contemplate on for a while, but what you're truly doing is working with the Savior to create a life of meaning and purpose.

How can I be more humble? I believe this is important to talk about because the scriptures and prophets tell us to humble ourselves. The scriptures tell us how, but I prefer to talk about it in layman's terms. I have shared some about letting go in the *Letting Go* chapter. Letting go is about accepting what may come no matter what. Humbleness is about accepting the Lord's will no matter what happens. Learning to let go of our masks and practice humbleness requires us to submit ourselves to the Lord mentally, spiritually, emotionally, and perhaps verbally. We stop kicking against the pricks and allow the Lord to guide us in the direction He wants us move toward, and then radically accept it. This takes practice and patience, just like many of these tools.

Practicing being humble will not be easy. You will have to let go of your masks. I promise as you let go of your masks and work on humbling yourself, you will feel freer and in control of yourself. It is an amazing feeling. It's kind of an oxymoron; the more you let go of control, the more control you have. As you develop the willingness to be humble, you are then on the right track to Godly Sorrow and true repentance, because Godly sorrow worketh repentance unto salvation. This will help you to break free from the shame of addiction. I guarantee it. You will feel more love from your Heavenly Father and Savior. You will feel worthy of love and belonging and know that you are still a work in progress. That is why we are here on earth; to learn and grow into eternal life.

CHAPTER 18

PRAYER AND FAITH

Okay, somehow you knew I was going to talk about prayer. It is only obvious since prayer has been a major component of human history as well as part of Church history and doctrine. Prayer is our channel and lifeline to our Heavenly Father. I have mentioned prayer previously and even shared my prayerful experiences. Prayer is how we communicate with our Father in Heaven through His Son Jesus Christ. In fact, Heavenly Father wants us to communicate with him anytime and anywhere. It is all part of His plan. I think it is amazing we can turn to Him whenever we want.

Prayer has been proven to be a wonderful tool that helps us in all sorts of ways. Research has determined that prayer helps people get better. Not only do people get better, but they can get better much faster than if they didn't pray (Colbert, 2017). It is interesting to learn that "[l]ong-term prayer can actually rewire and rebuild the brain" (Colbert, 2017). Remember when we were talking about building new neural pathways? This is exactly it! Prayer helps us to change the brain in creating new neural pathways and thus creating a more positive outlook! Dr. Colbert also shares various research indicating how prayer helps, from coping with asthma better to having lower blood pressure. Prayer is a tool that helps us feel better and grow mentally and spiritually.

Prayer is how we connect with God. God then connects with us through his Holy Spirit. If you are not praying, then I'm not sure if you can fully heal from your addiction and the shame that comes with it. Remember when we talked about connection. Connection is how we draw close to those we love. Connection helps us stay away from shame. The most important person we must connect with is our Savior.

But I've been praying and nothing has helped! So, you say. I read a story one time where the person had been praying for a miracle to happen in their life. It wasn't until 20 years later that their prayer was answered. Sometimes the Lord does not answer our prayers right away. Sometimes there are things that we must learn before He can bless us with what we need. I know this well. I have mentioned before that I have been blessed with the burden of financial hardships throughout the first 20 or so years of my marriage. This burden has been a blessing in disguise.

We lived in New Zealand for three years while my husband (Matt) worked on his PhD in Anthropology at the University of Waikato in Hamilton. It was an amazing experience. We were able to go because we had sold our house in Kansas (where he worked on his master's degree), which gave us the funds to be able to have such an adventure. New Zealand is not cheap, at least for a family making 20,000 New Zealand dollars a year. Our funds quickly evaporated, and we came back to the United States with no money, no home, no job, and no car to seat a family of eight. We had one small crate of our belongings and our suitcases. That was all. I had just finished my bachelor's degree that year and could have gotten a job, but I had a newborn baby to take care of. Matt was still working on his PhD dissertation, so that wasn't even finished.

We went back to Arizona to live with my husband's parents (which was only supposed to be for a short time). I felt trapped in their house with six children and no car to take them anywhere. It was torturous for me. My in-laws are wonderful people, but at that point I was not a wonderful person and found it extremely difficult to live with them. I mean, who doesn't want their own place so they could take care of their family? The problem was that Matt didn't have a job, so we couldn't rent a house. I felt trapped and stuck. I honestly thought we would only live at my in-laws for maybe two months, and I prayed diligently that my husband would get job so we could move out. However, it was not to be.

Five months in, I exploded and yelled at my mother-in-law. I felt terrible! I felt bad because here they were sharing their house with us. I decided to move two hours north to my dad's cabin. My dad let me borrow his car, which seated five people. Since we didn't have a car to seat everyone, I took my four youngest children and moved north. I cannot express the anxiety and depression I felt during the five months I was at my dad's cabin. I learned how to be a single mom, which was very scary. I oversaw four precious children under the age of nine. This was where I had a lot of dark moments too. I wanted to blame God for everything, because He was not answering my prayers—at least how I wanted them answered. I wallowed in my sorrow and "poor me" attitude. The one thing I never gave up on was prayer. I always knew God loved me. I knew he cared. There was a time when I was looking in the mirror and I heard the words in my head, "See, God doesn't really care about you." I knew it was Satan, and I quickly turned to prayer. It was a difficult time, but on the flip side, it was amazing in that I learned so many gospel truths and mysteries of God that I would have never had if I had not had that experience.

The situation did not get much better once summer hit. I knew my family wanted to use the cabin for the summer, so I packed up my little gang and drove back to my in-laws. I was there for two days when I realized I couldn't stay there. By this time, it had been 10 months since we came back from New Zealand. My husband was still unemployed and still working on his dissertation. I really had nowhere to go. I remember the Holy Spirit trying to comfort me, and I told it to go away. It did. I was so angry inside I didn't want to listen to anybody. I decided to pack up the three little kids and live out of the car—my dad's car. We spent the first night on the street nearby. It was June in Arizona. If you don't know, it's already 100 degrees or more during the day in Arizona. It was hot and uncomfortable. I don't think I slept at all. I remember crying all night long. We got up early, because the sun comes up at five in the morning in the summer. We then went to the grocery store and went inside to go to the bathroom and brush our teeth. I felt so humiliated.

I took the kids to the park to play until I could figure out what to do. I recall a nice elderly gentleman coming up to ask me if I was homeless. This only added to my humiliation. He said he has been homeless too and gave me some ideas on what I could do. None of them suited me at the time. I took the kids to the library next and from there decided I wasn't sleeping in the car anymore. I told my husband (mind you, he offered to come with me and go to a shelter, but I told him no), I was going to a motel and staying there. Thus, we began our crazy summer of homelessness. We spent nights at cockroach motels (seriously, they were gross), house sitting for friends, spending a week at my brother's house, and finding places where we could "crash" for the night. My son who was six years old then said, "This was the best summer ever!" I thought the contrary. There was one point during that summer where we were having family pictures for my in-laws. I recall my sister-in-law, who had put the whole thing together, say, "Oh, I'm so tired. I wish I could just go home and lie down." I had the stomach flu the day we took the pictures, and I wasn't feeling very well. I didn't let anyone know because I was pretty good at keeping it at bay. When I heard my sister-in-law say that, I ran into the other room and cried! At least she had a home!

This was my crazy year from the summer of 2012 to the summer of 2013. At the end of July 2013, Matt finally got a job, and we were able to get into a house. We still did not have a car to seat the whole family, but we had two cars that each sat five people. We had to drive two cars around everywhere for the next five years. Matt then lost his job two months after we moved into the house (it was a mortgage business) and then we had to look for work which took a long time as well. Meanwhile, Matt was still trying to finish his dissertation. Those were some of the most difficult years of my life. I don't think I could have made it through without the power of prayer. Prayer is what got me through those tough times. I prayed for years for my husband to finish his dissertation and get a job. It took him nine years total to finish his PhD. I prayed for nine years for him to finish and get a job. Sometimes we pray for things to happen, and they don't happen how we want them to happen. I may have not gotten my prayers answered the way I wanted them answered, but I did get them answered, and I learned so many things in the process. I do not think I would have ever learned the mysteries of God if He had answered my prayers right away. The question is not if God will answer our prayers, the question is what we can learn in the process of waiting for our prayers to be answered. "Ask, and it shall be given you; seek, and ye shall find; knock, and it shall be opened unto you: For every one that asketh receiveth; and he that seeketh findeth; and to him that knocketh it shall be opened" (Matthew 7:7-8). Sometimes we ask for good righteous things, but it may take a long time for us to receive it. This is where patience comes in, and where we look for and ask for things that will help us to learn and grow while we are patient for our answer.

It matters how you pray. It says in the scriptures, ". . . and if ye shall ask with a sincere heart, with real intent, having faith in Christ, he will manifest the truth of it unto you, by the power of the Holy Ghost" (Moroni 10:4). The key phrase is "real intent." Let us talk about what real intent means, because Heavenly Father may not answer your prayers if you don't have real intent. My definition of real intent is one who is genuinely interested and committed to the issue. It means that whatever the answer may be, you have a real desire to follow the Lord, and you have every intention of following Him. Do not forget that humbleness plays a huge role in your prayer. Real intent is also about being humble. This means you are humble enough to be patient and wait for when your answer will come.

Prayers are answered according to your faith. Faith is an amazing concept. Why is that? Because ". . . faith is not to have a perfect knowledge of things; therefore if ye have faith ye hope for things which are not seen, which are true" (Alma 32:21). Faith is hoping and believing that the Lord will answer your prayers. Faith is about being okay with whatever answer the Lord gives us.

While we were living in Arizona, after our finding a home ordeal, I worked on my master's degree and got my first job as a Substance Abuse Counselor at a women's treatment and trauma facility. Unfortunately, after 18 months of working there, the place shut down, and I needed a new job. I acquired two job offers, one of which I was overly excited about. I prayed about them, and the answer came as a "No." I needed to prepare myself and go to Colorado and look for a job there. I was distraught because my husband was still finishing his dissertation and had only a part-time job. I told my sister and dad what I needed to do. They told me not to go and to take the job that I was offered. I started to doubt myself, as things looked bleak. I prayed again, and again the answer was to go to Colorado. So, I did. It was scary, as I didn't know what to do and who I could stay with. I spent the first night in a motel. The next day was Sunday, and I was led by the Spirit to go to church at a certain ward. The ward family was very kind and inviting. I was lucky to find a couple that allowed me to stay at their house for an entire month. I spent my time searching for jobs and watching Downton Abbey—don't judge me. I had two job interviews (which I did not get) and when the month was up, I was ready to go home.

I cannot tell you how embarrassed I felt when I got home. I told everyone that the Spirit was leading me to Colorado, and I was looking for a job, and then I get home and . . . nothing. This was hard for me as I didn't understand God's logic in the whole process. There were many times when I wanted to give up and tell God, "Forget this, I'm sick and tired of trying to follow you, and I'm ready to do it my way!" Believe me, I wanted to do this as it felt like the easy way out. I knew better though. I knew I could not lose my faith in the Lord just yet. I was going to be patient and trust in Him.

Faith is a choice. It is not easy sometimes. I recall writing in my Journal back in 2014,

> Faith is not to have a perfect knowledge of things . . . Sometimes I get thoughts and feelings to 'just give it all up! Let go! The Gospel is just another . . . Same old; same old.' But I know these thoughts and feelings are not true. I hold on because I have faith. Faith in my Savior. When I have the former thoughts, I feel and sense confusion, but when I have faith, I feel and sense hope, understanding and light. So, I am holding on (Amanda Harms' Journal).

The key is to hold on and not give up. Faith is believing in what is true. Seeing is not always believing. Believing is definitely seeing, ". . . for ye receive no witness until after the trial of your faith" (Ether 12:6). When we believe in what is true, we can be assured that Heavenly Father will always answer our prayers and keep His promises. Please understand that when we pray in faith, we must keep our expectations open. I know there are many times where my prayers were answered but not according to my expectations. You can ask the Lord to make a horse fly, expecting to see the horse fly in the air, but maybe His way was getting a horse on a special plane that would fly the horse up into the sky. We must be careful of our expectations.

So, what happened to moving to Colorado? It turns out Matt got a job at the end of July with a community college and needed to move to Colorado in August. It was such short notice, but fortunately, we knew a family who instantly took him in. Yes, it was the same family who allowed me to stay a month at their house. I then was able to secure a job and begin working at the end of October. We had three weeks to pack up and move. As you can see, the Lord was preparing us for our move to Colorado.

As a person with an addiction, you might have prayed in faith and felt the Lord was not answering your prayers. You may have felt lonely, depressed, abandoned even because you continued to use. Prayer may feel like a one-way call with no one on the other end. But it doesn't have to. If we pray with faith, with "real intent," and doing our best, the Lord won't stay away. Our intent and our effort invite the Lord's help. We can pray in faith, believing, but if we aren't continuing to be committed and genuine in our intent, then how can the Lord help us? You have heard the phrase a million times: "Faith without works is dead" (James 2:20). We cannot give up! We need to continue to do what is required of us which includes keeping the commandments, reading the scriptures, prayer, taking the sacrament, fasting, as well as all that has been explained in this book. It is about taking care of ourselves mentally, physically, emotionally, and spiritually.

Please don't give up! The odds of the Lord helping you are amazingly good! There is a great book I used to read to my clients in group. It's called, *Oh The Places You'll Go,* by Dr. Seuss. Toward the end of the book, Dr. Seuss writes, "And you will succeed? Yes! You will indeed! (98 and ¾ percent guaranteed.) KID, YOU'LL MOVE MOUNTAINS!" (1990). Ninety-eight and three-fourths are rather good odds. I would bet the percentage is even higher when we have the Savior helping us! You can move this mountain of addiction and put it in its rightful place. Faith can move mountains. Believe you can, and you will!

Chapter 19

The Greatest Love Ever

I sure wish the English language had more than one word for "love." I feel the English language does not capture the different types of love well enough, not like the Greek language does. Usually, we have to say romantic love or brotherly love. In the Greek language, there are several different words for love that mean different things. The main three are: Eros which means romantic love, Philia which means friendship love, and Agape which is more of a selfless or unconditional love. In the *Bible*, Greek translations show that agape is used as the word for the love of God. This makes sense because Christ's love is unconditional and completely selfless. This means that no matter what you do or who you are, you are loved by the Savior. No. Matter. What.

The Savior's love is pure love. It has no conditions, no judgment. It is pure eternal love that will always be there for us. Sometimes we don't feel it because of our unrepentant souls. Sometimes we are so busy hiding behind our masks that we cannot feel His love reaching out to us. The Savior's love for you is so great. He can help you change your heart and guide you into the person He wants you to be if you allow Him to do so.

After the Passover, Jesus and three of his disciples went to Gethsemane. Gethsemane means "oil press" or "the place where oil is pressed." This is a fitting name for the place where the Savior performed His greatest act of love. Of course, this is where the infinite Atonement took place. You can look at the word atonement a couple of different ways. Atonement means to make reparations for any sinful or wrongful injustices. You can also see it as at-one-ment, where the person making the atonement becomes one with the person who has committed the injustice. The Savior, being perfect with no sin, loved you so much He suffered for you, so that you can become "one" with Him.

Think about it, there was a moment in history where the Savior thought only of you. As He suffered in the garden, He had one moment where He thought about you and your whole life. He knows you so intimately that He knows all of your pains, sufferings, sins, and sorrows. He knows your joys too. He knelt in the garden that night because of the great love He has for you! Sure, He did it for all mankind, but Jesus knows each of us individually, and He especially knows you.

If you have been to a courthouse, you may have seen a symbol of the Lady Justice. This is a blindfolded woman who is holding a set of scales. The type of scales where the items are weighed and balanced. They used these scales in the olden days to help make things fair in buying and selling various items. In the court system, it is a symbol of justice and mercy. There is another seminary video called *The Mediator*, filmed in 1993. It is on YouTube. I like how this short film explains the laws of justice and mercy.

In *The Mediator,* there was a man who borrowed money to buy a house and a farm. His intention was to farm the land, make money and pay his debt. Unfortunately, the man decided to go and "hang out" with his friends instead, and the work did not get done. The debt came due, and it was time for him to pay. The man told the debt collector he didn't have the money to pay. The debt collector told him that the man must go to jail. The man asked for mercy, but the debt collector asked for justice. Imagine if the debt collector gave mercy all the time. He would be out of business! It was fair of the debt collector to demand justice. Here is the dilemma, the man is in debt, but is *worth* having mercy given him, but the debt collector would be out of business if he did not stay true to justice. The man must go to jail to pay the justice, but where is mercy? If the debt collector gave mercy, then where is his justice?

We are the "man" who cannot pay the debt. Heavenly Father is somewhat like the debt collector. He must have justice paid for the sins we make. When we sin, we are in debt to Heavenly Father because he demands that justice be served for the sin. A price must be paid for our sins. "For I the Lord cannot look upon sin with the least degree of allowance" (D&C 1:31). In *The Mediator*, the man has a friend who comes and tells the debt collector that he will pay the debt. The friend tells the man that he will be in debt to him instead. The man was exceptionally grateful that his friend was merciful to him and satisfied the demands of justice so he would not have to go to jail. This friend of course represents our Savior, Jesus Christ. Can you imagine how grateful Heavenly Father is for Jesus? Heavenly Father loves us so much that He sent His son to satisfy the laws of justice, so that we can repent, receive mercy, and live with Him again. In Alma 42:15 it reads:

> And now, the plan of mercy could not be brought about except an atonement should be made; therefore God himself atoneth for the sins of the world, to bring about the plan of mercy, to appease the demands of justice, that God might be a perfect, just God, and a merciful God also.

Understanding why the atonement had to happen, we can see that Christ loved us enough to pay our debt for us! He suffered for us so that He could help us rise up from our carnal states and become more spiritually-minded. He suffered so that He would know how to "succor" us, or rather help us in our difficult times.

> And he will take upon him death, that he may loose the band of death which bind his people; and he will take upon him their infirmities, that his bowels may be filled with mercy, according to the flesh, that he may know according to the flesh how to succor his people according to their infirmities (Alma 7:12).

Christ's Atonement is the greatest love ever. I used to say in my prayers, *Father in Heaven, thank you for the Savior's Atonement.* Now I say, *Father in Heaven, thank you for the Savior and His great love He has for me.* The atonement was agape, pure unconditional love! Love is what brings the miracle of changed hearts. Love is what helps us to become humble and willing to keep the Lord's commandments. We follow the Savior because of how grateful we are and because of how much love we have for Him.

This means He knows exactly how to help you; physically, mentally, emotionally, and spiritually. I have a dear family member who gave me permission to share his story. I will call him Luke. Luke was raised with the Gospel taught in his home. His personality was such that he liked being independent and to do things his way. As a teenager, Luke shaved his head into a mohawk, wore dark colored clothing, and hung out with kids who were less than favorable from his parent's point of view. Luke began experimenting with drugs. He eventually stopped using around the time he was twenty-two years old. He got married and then the drug habit began again as his wife wanted to experiment with drugs. Luke got in so deep that one day he overdosed and had to go to the hospital. From his family's point of view, this was a turning point for Luke. Luke eventually got divorced from his wife. From there, things started to change. Luke became different in a good way. He started going to church and got his life back together. His mom told me a few times that Luke is a special spirit who always had a testimony of the Gospel and would come back to the Gospel. Luke eventually remarried in the Temple, which was an exciting time for his family. I thought it was amazing that the miracle of change had happened in his life, and it was all because of the Savior's Atonement, because of His love.

Luke's life was not easy after that though. He is not perfect, but he tried to do the best he could and stay true to the Gospel. His second marriage ended in divorce, and Luke felt a lot of shame because of it. He is now happily married again and continues to progress in the Gospel of Jesus Christ. I am immensely proud of Luke for staying sober all these years. Sometimes it is easy to go right back into drug use when trials get to be difficult. Luke's testimony of the Savior and His Atonement was able to help Luke get through the many trials he has faced. The Savior helped Luke understand things to help him get through his trials.

The Atonement or as I call it, Christ's Great Love, is able to soften hearts, enrich our minds with light and knowledge, produce love, produce peace, comfort us, and more if we allow it to work in our lives. I look at the Atonement as a gift from a dear friend. If we do not open the gift and use it, it is as if we don't care what our friend gave us. Our friend would be sad that we didn't use his gift. The Atonement is a gift from the Savior that we must use in our lives. It is what can help us get through life. Let's face it, life is hard. Wouldn't it be nice to have the great power of His love help us navigate life better?

The story of Moses raising the brass serpent comes to mind (Numbers 21). The Israelites had left Egypt and they were in the wilderness. They started complaining to Moses and God. God then sent fiery serpents to poison the people. He asked Moses to raise a serpent up on a pole and told Moses to tell the people to look at the brass serpent. If the people looked at it, then they would live from their poisonous snake bites. If they didn't look, then they would die. Many looked and lived, and many did not look, and they died.

I share this story because the way is so simple. All we need to do is look to Jesus and live. Look means to follow Him and do what He asks of us. Yet, we make it so difficult in our lives because of all the masks we put on. We allow the adversary to seep into our lives because it appears to be easier, and our brains love 'easy.' But was it easy for those Israelites who were bitten to die by poison compared to the Israelites who were bitten, looked up, and lived? The adversary wants you to believe his way is easier, and sometimes it is at first, but it is an illusion. You know this because taking that first drink, or line, or whatever it may be, is easy. After being in an addiction for a while, it's not easy. You lose your freedom. Going to church and feeling judged is hard. Remembering to read your scriptures daily and praying daily can be hard. Standing up to your friends who are gossiping about another friend is hard. The list goes on, however, over time following the Gospel of Jesus Christ becomes easier with practice. You will continue to have freedom to choose because you are not trapped by your addiction.

I always tell my children that the more difficult (bad) choices they make, the more freedoms they lose. The better choices they make, the more freedom they have to choose to make more "good" choices. For example, you decide to tell a lie to someone (I know we have all done it and perhaps some of us still do). You then loose the freedom of honesty and integrity. If that person finds out you lied, then you have lost the freedom of being trustworthy. No one will want to trust you because they know you have lied. It can take years to be trusted again. Then when you try to make connections with people, you cannot do it very easily. Your connections will be loose connections instead of tight ones. One lie. That is all it takes to lose some of your freedoms. I know someone who lied and ended up going to jail for it. Now their freedom is really lost.

I may have gotten off on a tangent, and I want to bring it back around to the Atonement. I share about choices because that is what it all comes down to—choices. You have the choice to make the hard decisions that will eventually become easy as you choose to continue to make those good decisions. The choice to use the Atonement in your life will benefit you more than you can imagine. I wish I could have shared this with my clients at work. I gave my clients many of the tools that I have shared in this book, but the greatest of all the tools is the Atonement of Jesus Christ.

The Savior's Atonement can help you break free from the shame of addiction and from your addiction itself. I am not saying you use the Atonement only, because the Lord helps those who help themselves. I am saying that as you use the tools I have talked about, the Lord can help ease your burden of addiction. He may not take it way completely, but He will give you the strength to keep working on your sobriety. The Lord can change your neural pathways in your brain in an instant, but what would you learn from that? The Lord knows that you must make the choice to work hard so you can change those neural pathways and work towards sobriety. He knows you will have a better understanding of how to get sober so you can help others with their sobriety. You can do this! The Lord believes in you and has never doubted you because He knows your great potential. He is reaching out to you and asking you to take His hand and experience the ride of His love. It is not going to be easy, but as you make better choices, you will empower yourself more each day. You will be able to overcome your weaknesses and draw closer to the Savior. It is a journey of progression, a journey of love, a journey self-realization, and you're doing it with your greatest friend—the Savior.

Chapter 20

Motivation

Now that you have the tools, you need to develop the skills. This takes practice along with staying motivated. Staying motivated is hard. Think about the New Year's resolutions you make. How many times have you stuck with those goals? You do well at first by going to the gym daily and eating well, but then life happens. Other priorities take its place and before you know it, you are too tired or not in the mood to go to the gym. Maybe you tell yourself this is the year you're going to quit your drug of choice. You start off strong and within the week, you are back at it again. Then you get down on yourself because you didn't stick with your goal and ultimately you dig yourself deeper in your addictive hole. We have all done this. Motivation takes work, and I want to share with you some techniques on how to stay motivated.

They say that Rome wasn't built in a day. You breaking free from your shame of addiction will take time. As one of my colleagues used to say, "Give yourself some grace." After all, you're only human; you are allowed to make mistakes. I know because I do it all the time. I used to get down on myself and feel the shame of my mistakes all the time. I would tell myself that I'm a bad person or a bad mother. I thought I needed to punish myself for all my mistakes. Then I went to school and learned how to understand myself. I changed my agreements with myself and gave myself an abundance of grace. I am not perfect, but I'm progressing.

To help stay motivated, I would hope you give yourself grace if you "fall off the band wagon." My dad calls it, "Falling off the turnip truck." We all do it. My husband's favorite movie is *Batman Begins* (2005). There is a part in the movie where Bruce Wayne falls into a well and breaks his arm. His dad comes and rescues him, and as he carries him in the house Thomas Wayne says to his son, "And why do we fall Bruce? So, we can learn to pick ourselves up" (Nolan, 2005). Heavenly Father allows us to fall, so that we can experience the learning of picking ourselves up again. It is how we learn. We learn from our failures and our mistakes. I know I have shared this previously, but I think it is very important to know that failures help us progress. Do we really fail if we are learning something from our failure, even if it is something small? No! We are progressing. We are motivated, then we fail, and we lose that motivation because we look at ourselves as failures instead of learners. This is what Satan wants us to believe, that we are failures. The result is that we stay in our shame. Well not anymore! Mistakes are a part of life, and we are learners, not failures!

Motivation is the drive to change and keeps us on the path of change. The reality is that change is hard because we have developed neural pathways in our brains that have become deeply ingrained so that we automatically go back to our old ways if something negative happens to us. "Your ability to find and maintain your motivation for meaningful and long-lasting change will ultimately determine whether you're able to break long-standing habits and patterns" (Taylor, 2012).

Motivation has many definitions. Dr. Jim Taylor gives some great definitions:

An internal or external drive that prompts a person to action;
The ability to initiate and persist toward a chosen objective;
Putting 100 percent of your time, effort, energy, and focus into your goal attainment;
The determination to resist ingrained unhealthy patterns and habits;
Doing everything you can to make the changes you want in your life;
Facing obstacles, boredom, fatigue, stress, and the desire to do other things.

Which definition suits you currently? Maybe you have more than one. The purpose of staying motivated is the "why" you want to act. I want you to make a list of the "whys" when it comes to your goals. This is especially the case when learning to break free from your shame. Maybe you want to practice being more positive, or work on being more mindful. The "whys" are important, and I hope you write them down and put them somewhere where you can see them daily to help remind you of your motivation to work on your goals.

Dr. Taylor gives us the four "P's" of motivation: Preparation, Patience, Persistence, and Perseverance. First, you have to prepare. If you are running a race, you've got to start slow and work your way to running faster. Patience requires you to give "yourself time for changes to occur" (Taylor, 2012). You cannot run one mile today and five miles the next day. It takes time. Persistence requires you to be mindful of when you go back into your old habits and ways of doing things. When you are mindful, you can redirect yourself back to your goal. Lastly, perseverance is working your way through the obstacles. This is also part of what Dr. Taylor calls "The Grind."

There are going to be times when you put in the work for change, but it becomes uninspiring. It feels as if you have reached a brick wall and it doesn't feel fun anymore (Taylor, 2012). For some people, this feeling may come within two or three days of trying to change, or it may come in a couple of months. Dr. Taylor calls this "The Grind, which starts when actions necessary to produce meaningful change becomes stressful, tiring, and tedious" (2012). This is when we need to persevere. I find it most helpful to turn to the Lord in these instances when we just don't have "it" in us to keep progressing in our change. You don't have to like "The Grind," but you don't have to hate it either. When we "hate" things, the negative feeling works towards keeping us from staying motivated to change. We practice radical acceptance of "The Grind" to help us stay in the "motivation zone." "The Grind" does not feel good. During these times, we need to remember that life doesn't always feel good, and usually when we "feel good," we are not growing. "The Grind" helps us to push through and continue our growth towards change.

A good quality to attain when trying to change is *consistency*. Consistency is one of the keys to maintaining quality change. Consistency is what helps us to change those neural pathways in our brains. If you fall off the turnip truck, it's okay. You pick yourself back up and keep on being consistent with your progress. Don't beat yourself up for falling off. Okay, you are allowed to do it once, but then give yourself a positive talk and keep going. You can do this!

Dr. Angela Duckworth is a researcher who studies "grit." In fact, she wrote a book on grit called, *Grit: The Power of Passion and Perseverance*

(2016). Grit is "firmness of mind or spirit: unyielding courage in the face of hardship or danger" (Merriam-Webster, *Grit*). When I think of professional athletes, I think of "grit." Professional athletes have the courage to keep going—to get stronger and better in their profession. Grit is part of "The Grind." We must develop "grit" if we are going to pull through "The Grind" and stay motivated. If you are curious about your own "grit," Dr. Duckworth has developed a grit scale. You can find this scale at: https://angeladuckworth.com/grit-scale/. I encourage you to try it out. Like everything, grit takes practice. Start with the small things and work your way up. You will find that your courage to face hardships will increase, and you will find it easier to stay motivated.

The key to motivation is mindfulness. Yes, you probably knew I was going to mention that again. Mindfulness, learning to be in the moment, is what helps you to stay focused on change. Being mindful of yourself is probably one of the greatest gifts you can give yourself. If you are mindful of how you feel physically, then you can take the steps to help yourself feel better. If you are mindful of your feelings, then you can take the steps to understand those feelings and better understand yourself. If you are mindful of your behaviors, then you can take the necessary steps to change those behaviors for the better. If you are mindful of your spirituality, then you can take the steps to be closer to your Savior and feel His love that He has for you. Mindfulness is a superpower. Don't take it for granted because it is the main key to change.

Also, don't take for granted the power of the Savior's love that He has for you. When you feel burdened by your addiction and the shame of it, you always have the Savior who can lift you up and help you stay motivated. When you feel like using, turn to the Lord. When you feel low and tired of it all, turn to the Lord. When you feel like you can't go on, turn to the Lord. Sometimes we feel like He is not answering us, so we give up and turn back to our addiction. Please, do not give up on the Lord, because He's not giving up on you. Hold on, and the light will come. Hold on, and He will answer. Hold on, and you will see change in your life. Hold on, and you will see miracles in your life!

It is hard to stay motivated in these human bodies. Our human brains like comfort and ease. It is so easy to just forget about change and go back into our old ways of doing things. I like Sheri Dew's book, *If Life were Easy, It Wouldn't Be Hard and Other Reassuring Truths* (2005). Sister Dew shares that life is meant to be hard. We cannot win a marathon or reach the top of

Mount Everest without the 4 "Ps" and getting through the grind. Moreover, we cannot be perfected like Christ and live with Him again unless we work with Him by using our skills and the tools we've learned about in this book. Remember, it is progression. We fall, pick ourselves back up again, and keep going. We sin and make mistakes. We choose to follow the Savior and allow His Atoning sacrifice to work in our lives to help us become perfected someday. It may not be in this life, but it will happen, as we choose to follow the Savior.

CHAPTER 21

TODAY IS THE FIRST DAY OF
THE REST OF YOUR LIFE!

Today *is* the first day of the rest of your life, and you can now move forward with more faith and determination to create a new you. You are becoming a person who has the skills to break free from the shame of your addiction and ultimately break free from addiction itself. In reality, you are changing yourself to become a whole new person. In 2 Corinthians 5:17 it reads, "Therefore if any man be in Christ, he is a new creature: old things are passed away; behold, all things are become new." As we draw closer to the Savior, we each become a new person. We put off the natural man or woman and become a spiritual man or woman. We are no longer carnally-minded, but spiritually-minded.

I genuinely hope you will take the time to understand more about shame and addiction; especially how shame affects your addiction. I hope you will practice the tools given in this book. It will not be easy. Anything worthwhile takes patience, time, and dedication. Realize that the process of breaking free from shame will take some time. In essence, you are changing neural pathways, which take months to change, maybe even years. You are also changing your carnal mind into a spiritual mind. You are fighting against the fiery darts of the adversary as you grow spiritually strong. You are developing a personal relationship with your Savior and learning to love yourself as He loves you. Wow, that is an amazing concept; loving yourself as the Savior loves you!

109

Part of learning to love yourself is taking care of yourself: mentally, spiritually, physically, and emotionally. I admit that I might be a bit selfish because I always put myself first when it comes to these aspects of my being. I do this because I realize how important it is for me to take care of myself before I can truly take care of others. I believe you cannot truly take care of others if you don't take care of yourself first. Think about it, if you are not one hundred percent, then others aren't getting all that you can give when you are at one hundred percent capacity. I may be selfish in a way, but I'm able to give more because I have more within me. I encourage you to write down your goals (hopefully they include the tools I have shared in this book), and then work on achieving them. Again, use the workbook provided on my website. Work through the grind, pray, and ask for help. If you fall, you fall. It's okay. Just pick yourself back up again and keep going. If you keep at it, you will progress and eventually succeed. You will never be perfect in this life, but you can be perfect in little things. It all adds up.

Most importantly, I encourage you to study more about the Savior's great love for you. His great, infinite Atonement is the greatest gift we could ever receive. He suffered in the garden, on the cross, and then He died for *us*. He was perfect and without sin. He didn't have to do what He did, but because He was perfect and loved us so much, He suffered and died for us. Christ knew we would sin and would never be able to live with Him if the price wasn't paid, and because He was perfect, He paid the ultimate price for us. There is no sin, other than denying the Holy Ghost, that Christ cannot overcome. You are worthy of His love. You are worthy of belonging to Him because *you are* a precious child of God.

The message of the Savior is the most important message I want to give you, as it gives us faith and hope in the eternal plan of happiness. It is a message of Love. I hope you will also work on finding more love in your life and more compassion for yourself. Compassion and love are some of the greatest gifts you can give yourself. Do this daily. Every time you have a negative thought about yourself or make a mistake, try not beat yourself up over it, but rather send it love and compassion. As you work on this, you will feel the love of your Savior; the great love He has for you. You will know that you are worth love and belonging. You will no longer feel the shame. You will feel the desire to do better because of your love for the Savior. You will finally break free from your shame of addiction, and you will grow in love and understanding not only for yourself but for others as well. You can then be a light to others and spread the greatest love ever!

Bibliography

Act for Themselves (1993) - YouTube. (2016, January 8) https://www.youtube.com/watch?v=z1n1UoDlTzI

Alcoholics Anonymous World Services, Inc. (2016). *Twelve Steps and Twelve Traditions.*

Amen, D. G. (1998). *Change Your Brain, Change Your Life: the Revolutionary, Scientifically Proven Program for Conquering Anxiety, Depression, Obsessiveness, Anger, and Impulsiveness.* Times Books.

American Psychiatric Association. (2022). *Diagnostic and Statistical Manual of Mental Disorders* (5th ed.). https://doi.org/10.1176/appi.books.9780890425596

Benson, E.T. (1989, May). *Ensign: Beware of Pride.* The Church of Jesus Christ of Latter-Day Saints. https://www.churchofjesuschrist.org/study/ensign/1989/05/beware-of-pride?lang=eng

Brown, B. (2010). *The Gifts of Imperfection: Let Go of Who You Think You're Supposed To Be and Embrace Who You Are.* Hazelden Publishing.

Brown, B. (2012). *Daring Greatly: How the Courage To Be Vulnerable Transforms the Way We Live, Love, Parent, and Lead.* Penguin.

Castro, A. (2016). *What's Your Communication Style?* Communication Style Quiz. https://amycastro.com/wp-content/uploads/2017/09/Communication-Style-Quiz.pdf

The Church of Jesus Christ of Latter-Day Saints (1995, September 23). *The Family: A Proclamation to the World.* Salt Lake City, UT.

The Church of Jesus Christ of Latter-day Saints. (1999). *The Book of Mormon: Another Testament of Jesus Christ; The Doctrine and Covenants of the Church of Jesus Christ of Latter-day Saints; The Pearl of Great Price.*

The Church of Jesus Christ of Latter-day Saints. (2005). *Addiction Recovery Program: a Guide to Addiction Recovery and Healing.*

Colbert, D. (2019, February 26). *The Stunning Science Behind the Healing Power of Prayer*. Dr. Don Colbert. https://drcolbert.com/the-stunning-science-behind-the-healing-power-of-prayer/

Covey, S. R. (2013). *The 7 Habits of Highly Effective People*. Simon & Schuster UK Ltd.

Dew, S. L. (2005). *If Life Were Easy, It Wouldn't Be Hard: and Other Reassuring Truths*. Deseret Book.

Duckworth, A. (2016). *Grit: The Power of Passion and Perseverance*. Scribner.

The Four Basic Styles of Communication. https://www.uky.edu/hr/sites/www.uky.edu.hr/files/wellness/images/Conf14_FourCommStyles.pdf

Fredrickson, B. L. (2009). *Positivity: Top-notch Research Reveals the 3-to-1 Ratio That Will Change Your Life*. Three Rivers Press/Crown Publishers.

Hawkins, D. R. (2018). *Letting Go: the Pathway of Surrender*. Hay House, Inc.

Hawthorne, N. (1850). *The Scarlet Letter*. Ticknor and Fields.

Holland, J. R. (2012, April) *The Laborers in the Vineyard*. The Church of Jesus Christ of Latter-Day Saints. https://www.churchofjesuschrist.org/study/general-conference/2012/04/the-laborers-in-the-vineyard?lang=eng

"It's So Incredible To Finally Be Understood." 16 Personalities. https://www.16personalities.com/

King James Bible. (2021). King James Bible Online. https://www.kingjamesbibleonline.org/ (Original work published 1769).

Kolk, B. A. van der. (2015). *The Body Keeps the Score: Mind, Brain and Body in the Transformation of Trauma*. Penguin Books.

Kubler-Ross, E. (2003). *On Death and Dying: What the Dying Have To Teach Doctors, Nurses, Clergy, and Their Own Families*. Scribner.

Leonard, J. (2019, July 11). *EMDR Therapy: Benefits, Effectiveness, and Side Effects*. Medical News Today. https://www.medicalnewstoday.com/articles/325717?back=https%3A%2F%2Fwww.google.com%2Fsearch%3Fclient%3Dsafari%26as_qdr%3Dall%26as_occt%3Dany%26safe%3Dactive%26as_q%3Dwhat%27s%2Bthe%2Beffectiveness%2Brate%2Bof%2Ba%2BEMDR%26channel%3Daplab%26source%3Da-app1%26hl%3Den#benefits.

Linehan, M. (2014). *DBT Skills Training: Handouts and Worksheets*. GUILFORD Press.

Love Lab. The Gottman Institute. (2019, September 10). https://www.gottman.com/love-lab/

Bibliography

The Mediator (1993) - YouTube. (2016, January 8). https://www.youtube.com/watch?v=d7N5QDDboi8

Melemis, S. (2020, December 21). *The Genetics of Drugs and Alcohol Addiction.* I Want to Change My Life. https://www.addictionsandrecovery.org/is-addiction-a-disease.htmp

Merriam-Webster. (n.d.). *Grit.* Merriam-Webster. https://www.merriam-webster.com/dictionary/grit

Merriam-Webster. (n.d.). *Victim.* Merriam-Webster. https://www.merriam-webster.com/dictionary/victim

Nolan, C. (Director). (2012). *Batman Begins* [Film on DVD]. Warner Bros.

Packer, B. K. (2010, October) *Cleansing the Inner Vessel.* The Church of Jesus Christ of Latter-Day Saints. https://www.churchofjesuschrist.org/study/general-conference/2010/10/cleansing-the-inner-vessel?lang=eng

Ruth, A. (2015, July 22). *Thomas Edison - 10,000 Ways That Won't Work.* Due. https://due.com/blog/thomas-edison-10000-ways-that-wont-work/

Smith, E. E. (2020, May 11). *The Secret to Love Is Just Kindness.* The Atlantic. https://www.theatlantic.com/health/archive/2014/06/happily-ever-after/372573/

Suess, Dr. (1990). *Oh, the Places You'll Go!* Random House.

Taylor, J. (2012, January 2). *Personal Growth Motivation: The Drive to Change.* Psychology Today. https://www.psychologytoday.com/us/blog/the-power-prime/201201/personal-growth-motivation-the-drive-change

TED. (2014, November 24). *Kasim Al-Mashat: How Mindfulness Meditation Redefines Pain, Happiness, and Satisfaction* [Video]. YouTube. https://www.youtube.com/watch?v=JVwLjC5etEQ.

TED. (2015, July 9). *Johann Hari: Everything You Think You Know about Addiction Is Wrong* [Video]. YouTube. https://www.ted.com/talks/johann_hari_everything_you_think_you_know_about_addiction_is_wrong

Uchtdorf, D. F. (2010, October). *Pride and the Priesthood.* The Church of Jesus Christ of Latter-Day Saints. https://www.churchofjesuschrist.org/study/general-conference/2010/10/pride-and-the-priesthood?lang=eng

Uchtdorf, D. F. (2013, October). *You Can Do It Now.* The Church of Jesus Christ of Latter-Day Saints. https://www.churchofjesuschrist.org/study/general-conference/2013/10/you-can-do-it-now?lang=eng

Wilcox, B. (2013). *The Continuous Conversion.* Deseret Book Company.

Ziskin, L., & Schulman, T. (Directors). (1991). *What about Bob?* [Film on DVD]. Buena Vista Pictures Distribution, Inc.

About the Author

Amanda Harms was born and raised in Mesa, Arizona. She met her husband while taking a psychology class at college, and a year later, they were married. Her main job consisted of raising their children while her husband attended school. After twelve years of being absent from school, Amanda chose to obtain her bachelor's degree in Psychology from Liberty University. She continued her studies at Ottawa University obtaining a master's degree in Counseling and is currently working toward her Ph.D. in Social Psychology. Amanda had the opportunity to work with both men and women in clinical settings such as domestic violence, anger management, parenting groups, and addiction. She has worked with both men women at residential treatment facilities teaching mindfulness meditation, emotion regulation, stress tolerance, and vulnerability. She's also had the experience of working as a Neurofeedback Technician which allowed her to study the brain more fully. She currently works as a mental health counselor. Amanda has been fortunate enough to live in different places including Arizona, Kansas, and New Zealand. She currently lives with her husband and 6 children in Colorado.

Use the Q4 Code to Visit

https://www.lovenlifebyamanda.org/